THE GREAT FIRE

Kit Brookman

Currency Press, Sydney

BELVOIR

CURRENT THEATRE SERIES

First published in 2016
by Currency Press Pty Ltd,
PO Box 2287, Strawberry Hills, NSW, 2012, Australia
enquiries@currency.com.au
www.currency.com.au
in association with Belvoir, Sydney.

Cataloguing-in-publication data for this title is available from the National
Library of Australia website: www.nla.gov.au

Typeset by Dean Nottle for Currency Press.
Cover design by Alphabet Studio.
Front cover shows, from left, Sandy Gore, Genevieve Picot, Geoff Morrell,
Sarah Armanious and Peter Carroll (with Lucky Jim). (Photo by Brett Boardman)

Currency Press acknowledges the Traditional Owners of the Country on which
we live and work. We pay our respects to all Aboriginal and Torres Strait
Islander Elders, past and present.

Contents

The Great Fire was first produced at Belvoir St Theatre, Sydney, on 6 April 2016, with the following cast:

HANNAH	Sarah Armanious
DONALD	Peter Carroll
MARY	Lynette Curren
MICHAEL	Eden Falk
ALISON	Sandy Gore
LILY	Shelly Lauman
TOM	Marcus McKenzie
PATRICK	Geoff Morrell
ALEX	Yalin Ozucelik
JUDITH	Genevieve Picot

Director, Eamon Flack
Set Designer, Michael Hankin
Costume Designer, Jennifer Irwin
Lighting Designer, Damien Cooper
Composer and Sound Designer, Steve Francis
Associate Sound Designer, Michael Toisuta
Assistant Set Designer, Charles Davis
Stage Managers, Mel Dyer and Luke McGettigan
Assistant Stage Manager, Gina Bianco

CHARACTERS

MARY, early 80s
DONALD, early 80s, Mary's husband
PATRICK, around 60, their son
JUDITH, around 60, married to Patrick

Their children:
LILY, mid 30s
ALEX, early 30s
TOM, mid 20s

and
HANNAH, married to Alex
MICHAEL, married to Lily
ALISON, a neighbour, a visual artist, around 60

SETTING

Australia, the present day. The action takes place between December 23rd and New Year's Day at Judith and Patrick's house in the Adelaide Hills.

NOTES

'/' symbol indicates an interruption; the point at which the next line is begun.
If there is an interval it should come between Acts Two and Three.

This play went to press before the end of rehearsals and may differ from the play as performed.

ACT ONE: ARRIVAL

The interior of a large, ramshackle house in semi-rural Australia. A large kitchen/dining/living room—the kitchen/dining half stage left, and living room stage right. One door, downstage left, leads outside to the front yard. Another, a large wooden door, leads to another room (the dining room) upstage right. A smaller door upstage leads out into a corridor that in turn leads to the rest of the house and, beyond that, the garden.

The house has been built in the 1970s by amateur house builders, with absolute tenderness and love. It is not modern, or pristine, or neat, or even necessarily clean, but it is achingly beautiful.

It is late morning, on December the 23rd.

The sunlight is not harsh Australian sunlight. It gives things colour, rather than flattens them out.

LILY, *thirties, tall, contained, serious-faced, alert, sits, perched precariously on the arm of one of the couches, holding a vase filled with withered roses. She sits there for a while until* MICHAEL, *her husband, a man who speaks louder than he needs to, enters.*

MICHAEL: What are you doing?

LILY: Sorry.

MICHAEL: I thought you were in the garden, I've been looking for you.

LILY: I was in the middle of throwing these out and I got stuck.

MICHAEL: Stuck?

LILY: They're wilted, aren't they?

MICHAEL: Yeah.

LILY: They're really past it.

MICHAEL: I think so.

LILY: I hoped they might have a day left in them.

MICHAEL: What made you get stuck?

LILY: I was just thinking.

MICHAEL: Well, I've been looking for you.

LILY: Sorry.

MICHAEL: You've got me working out there, it's very hot, you know, and you're in here thinking about flowers.

LILY: I wasn't thinking about flowers.

MICHAEL: What's the time?

LILY: Nearly midday.

MICHAEL: Then they'll be here soon.

LILY: Soon-ish.

MICHAEL: Were you thinking about how you're going to ask them?

LILY: What? No.

MICHAEL: I thought we agreed that you were going to ask them.

LILY: I think we talked about it in passing, I don't think that we agreed.

MICHAEL: You have to ask them.

LILY: I'll mention it. If there's the right moment.

MICHAEL: Even just ten bucks less a week. I think it will make a real difference.

LILY: The rent's already cheap. Very.

MICHAEL: But we've got the upkeep of this place, which takes up a lot of time. A lot of time that we could be working on more important—

LILY: Yeah, I'll—if there's a moment, I—

MICHAEL: And let's be honest, Lil, they can afford it.

LILY: They already let us have this place at a fraction—

MICHAEL: But we can't afford it, we can't afford it, Lil, and having us in here is good for them, do you remember the last time they actually had tenants here, how that ended up, how that fat child with emotional problems put rocks down the toilet and fucked the sewage? You have to ask.

LILY: If there's a moment, I'll ask.

MICHAEL: I remember the first time I met your parents, I was terrified, completely terrified, and now they're coming to our house for Christmas.

LILY: Their house, that we rent from them.

MICHAEL: There I was, some twenty-six-year-old nobody, already professionally intimidated by your dad—and your mum, these two significant artists, and I'm sleeping with their only daughter, and the first thing out of my mouth, my first remark, was telling your mother she had muscly hands because her handshake had nearly snapped my fingers. She didn't take it well, either, we all tried to laugh it off but the undercurrent was palpable, it was, 'This guy is an irredeemable jerk'.

LILY: Well, then, they came around. And you're not nobody now, are you?

MICHAEL: The first thing I did was insult your mother. Unintentionally. But, I mean, why should it be an insult, anyway, or awkward, it's just an observation, some people have muscly hands, I didn't have any sort of pejorative tone when I said it, for all they knew I might have thought that a firm handshake was the best, sexiest thing ever.

LILY: You were a little bit insulting.

MICHAEL: Actually, I don't think I was, it was the circumstances that turned my observation into something awkward, that has retrospectively become insulting, but really, in the moment, if we'd all been able to suspend our awkwardness, our fear that we might inadvertently insult each other in the course of conversation, an otherwise completely innocuous conversation, anodyne even, then no-one would even remember it.

LILY: I think that my mum might remember it.

MICHAEL: Not if she wasn't so self-conscious about it.

LILY: Anyway, it doesn't—

MICHAEL: It's that sort of thing, you know, personal … hang-ups that get in the way of just trying to actually have a real, a real interaction with—it's a very Australian thing that we do, it's not like that in Europe, the thing about Australia—

LILY: I'll chuck these out, shall I?

She goes out the front door, and leaves the stage, taking the wilted flowers. MICHAEL *follows her to the front door and keeps talking to her from the doorstep.*

MICHAEL: I mean that's what interests me about this next project, this play is all about that sort of thing, how we allow personal squeamishness to intrude on relationships that should—that have the potential to be actually, like pure—well, nothing is pure, but honest! I think it might be the best thing I've ever read, that I've worked on anyway, it's like every time I read it some new facet reveals itself to me. Of course it's got its flaws, I just mean—of the plays that I've worked on in the past, I think it's the best, but then I haven't directed *Hamlet* yet, there's a lot of plays I haven't directed.

LILY *comes back in.*

But it's the reason I'm most excited about—you threw them out?

LILY: Yes, I thought—

MICHAEL: They'd have been fine for another day or two.

LILY: We just—

MICHAEL: You just cut the stems, you know, and that revitalises them. It's a shame to not have any flowers. How long do we have until they arrive?

LILY: They said early afternoon, so they could be here any—

MICHAEL: There's that place in Dorset Vale, those people who leave bunches of flowers by the side of the road, you could nip down there.

LILY: I'll just get some from the garden.

MICHAEL: Are you kidding? Your dad will lose it if anyone meddles with the garden.

LILY: I'm not going to Dorset Vale.

MICHAEL: Touch his garden and he'll *increase* the rent as punishment.

LILY: Fine, no flowers.

MICHAEL: We're not ready, all that stuff has to go into the cellar, I was going to fix the light fitting in their room as well.

LILY: The light fitting?

MICHAEL: Yeah, I tried to switch one of the lamps on and it kind of popped out of the wall, the wiring's visible.

LILY: It popped out?

MICHAEL: I might have knocked it a bit.

LILY: This bloody house, every single day something falls apart. One day we'll just be sitting here in this room and without warning the roof will cave in on us. We should bring up those things from the fridge in the laundry, I think there's still some stuff in the boot of the car as well, could you get that?

She starts to go out. He follows her.

MICHAEL: You still have to ask them about lowering the rent, I can't take on any more projects this year, I've got no time to find other work, I've got hardly any prep time for *Doll's House* as it is.

He comes back and gets a beer from the fridge.

LILY: Why are you drinking?

MICHAEL: It's Christmas. I have to get through it somehow.

They leave the stage.

After a while, TOM, *early twenties, comes through the front door carrying an old suitcase. He's a small, skinny, odd-looking jumble of a person with a bearing that slips quickly between being very guarded and very open. He looks at the house, taking in every detail. After a little while he sets down his suitcase next to one of the couches, where he has a good view of the front door. He pauses briefly, then sits on top of the suitcase and waits.*

After a while, we hear LILY *and* MICHAEL *approaching. They sound as if they're in a hurry. When they enter, they're carrying shopping.*

I just don't remember them saying that they were arriving today.

LILY: Well, they said it.

MICHAEL: To you, maybe, but you didn't tell me, not until this morning. I knew there was a thing tomorrow, I was ready for that.

LILY: Really? What had you done to get ready for that?

MICHAEL: Psychologically ready, I mean, I had steeled myself.

LILY: And you were going to leave the mundane details to me?

MICHAEL: I was going to do what you told me to do, they're your family, I said we could spend Christmas with mine, it would have been a lot less stressful.

LILY: We spent Christmas with them last year.

MICHAEL: Exactly, we've had recent practice with them. And you actually get on with my family, they're not suspicious of you the way your family is suspicious of me.

LILY: Tom!

TOM: Hi.

LILY *runs to him and hugs him.*

MICHAEL: Hi, Tom.

TOM: Hi, Michael.

MICHAEL: What a useless suitcase.

TOM: It's just old.

MICHAEL: Why would you have one like that when you could get one that was superior in every way, like actually practical, you could have one with wheels.

LILY: When did you get here?

TOM: Just a minute ago.

MICHAEL: Instead of a sort of faded hipster thing that …

> *Realising no-one is listening to him,* MICHAEL *dwindles.*

LILY: We were just down the back, in the laundry. We didn't see your car, I didn't hear you.

TOM: I parked up the hill a little way.

LILY: Are Mum and Dad here?

TOM: If they are I haven't seen them.

LILY: Look at you.

TOM: Look at you.

MICHAEL: I'll put this stuff away then, shall I?

LILY: When did you get back?

TOM: Yesterday. To Melbourne. I flew here this morning.

LILY: Melbourne? But you'll go back to Sydney after Christmas?

TOM: I guess so, if Mum and Dad will have me. I don't have anywhere else to live. I saw Gwen while I was in Melbourne, she said to say hi—she's not coming back here this year.

LILY: Really? That's a first. Alison and Richard will be disappointed.

TOM: Well, we've reached that point, haven't we, it's not automatic that we all come back here for Christmas. Well, maybe it still is for some of us.

LILY: Some of us are already here. It's so good to see you.

MICHAEL: Where did you want this stuff, Lil?

LILY: Which room do you want?

TOM: Oh, God, I don't know. My old room, I guess.

MICHAEL: Yeah, sorry, I've kind of been using it as my office so it's a bit messy, we just hadn't quite got to it yet.

LILY: We didn't know whether or not to expect you this year.

TOM: Yeah, I wasn't sure if I'd come. Mum insisted, I buckled.

LILY: Well, I'm glad you're here. It's good to have you home again.

MICHAEL: How long since you've been here?

TOM: Oh, years. Maybe three years, I think. To this house.

LILY: That long?

TOM: Time flies.

LILY: Stay as long as you like.

TOM: Thanks. I had thought that I would stay a little while. Until after New Year's, at least, then back to …

LILY: Great. Yes. Please.

TOM: Back to Sydney. I'll take this upstairs then.

LILY: Okay. We've got to keep getting ready, but you just relax.

MICHAEL: Have a beer if you want.

LILY: Or a cup of tea?

TOM: Cup of tea would be lovely, thanks.

How strange to be home.

He goes out. Slight pause.

MICHAEL: We did know he was coming, didn't we?

LILY: Mum wasn't sure.

MICHAEL: He looks like he's swallowed a small hive of bees. Why does he have that ridiculous suitcase? It looks like it weighs more than he does.

LILY: We should try to fix up the garden a bit before Mum and Dad get here.

MICHAEL: It looks fine.

LILY: He looks so grown-up.

MICHAEL: Not really, Lily.

LILY: To me he does.

MICHAEL: Well, he's your youngest brother.

LILY: I'm glad he's here.

MICHAEL: How long was he overseas for?

LILY: Since June I think. Mum's been worried about him.

MICHAEL: Why?

LILY: Look, I'll … tell you later.

MICHAEL: Just tell me now, he can't hear.

LILY: I know this house better than you, Michael, I know when people can—I'll tell you in the garden, come on, we've got to make it like we at least made an effort.

They start to go outside.

Oh, cup of tea.

She hits the button on the kettle, takes out a teacup and drops a teabag in it.

MICHAEL: It's going to be stinking hot today, you know. I thought we were past it when we got through that week above forty, but no.

They go out the front door.

After a moment, TOM *re-enters. He goes to the window, pushes aside one of the curtains, looks out. The kettle finishes boiling, but he doesn't move. He stays like this a little moment, then shakes his head quickly and goes to the kettle.*

ALISON *enters. She is carrying a tray of fruit mince pies.*

ALISON: Knock-knock! Tom! Hello, dear. I'm just being a nosy neighbour.

TOM: Ally! Come in.

ALISON: What a nice surprise to see you here. I'm bringing some Christmas treats. They're fruit mince pies. I was just going to leave them on the windowsill but there's a magpie up on the top lawn that was watching me beadily every step I took, and I thought that if I left them outside, he'd have them.

TOM: Thank you.

ALISON: They're just out of the oven so they might need to cool down. Are Lily and Michael about?

TOM: They're just out in the garden I think.

ALISON: That's not like them.

TOM: Trying to make it presentable.

ALISON: Oh, I see. For the house inspection. We have no such assistance around the house this year, our offspring are all staying put where they are.

TOM: Gwen said. I saw her, in Melbourne.

ALISON: Oh, good. Is it today that your mum and dad are arriving?

TOM: Yeah, they should be here soon actually, if you wanted to—

ALISON: I've got to be getting back, I've got lots of things on the go, I'm on a very strict timetable. Richard's back is playing up so he's lying on it, laid up, so I've got twice the scurrying around to do this year. If Lily and Michael start to look faint with hunger these might sustain them. You've been overseas. Lily was telling me.

TOM: Yeah.

ALISON: You were gone for a while.

TOM: Six months.

ALISON: Where were you?

TOM: All over. I ended up in Sweden for quite a while.

ALISON: Oh, wonderful.

TOM: And how are you?

ALISON: Oh, much the same, dear. We have a new rooster. From Spain. An Andalusian Blue. Quite a dark-feathered stocky fellow with a big comb and wonderful red jowls. But he and Norman, our old rooster, don't like each other very much, they had a couple of scrapes to begin with, so Richard has had to split our chook pen down the middle so they've each got a bit of territory. Carlos—he's our Andalusian—would probably think of it as divide and conquer. So getting that set up has taken quite some time, it's a very elaborate chook pen now, thoroughly fox-proof. One person has referred to it as Fowlcatraz. First thing in the morning Norman and Carlos will be up crowing, a kind of rooster-y harmonising. You'll probably hear them tomorrow.

TOM: Yes.

ALISON: Now listen, Tom, I have some things of yours tucked away in our house, they're stashed under the stairs, with the dogs. They're some board games, and some little pictures drawn on cardboard that you and our girls made when you were younger.

TOM: Oh.

ALISON: I don't know when they were made, before you moved away, so maybe when—how old were you when you moved away?

TOM: Thirteen.

ALISON: Yes. So maybe you made these when you were about eleven. You've hardly been back since you left, have you? I don't have a clear idea of the rules of the board games. Occasionally I catch our dogs looking at them quizzically, but I don't think they've been able to decipher them yet either. I found them when we were clearing out one of the attics, these wonderful little drawings, and I thought that you should have them. I'll make sure to bring them over this evening if I get a moment, or you drop by and get them tomorrow if you like.

TOM: Alright.

ALISON: I'm just going to steal one of my own gifts, just to make sure they're alright.

She takes a fruit mince pie. Bites into it.

There we are. Proof they're not poisoned. I'll see you tomorrow.

TOM: 'Bye. Thanks for the treats.

ALISON: That's alright, dear.

MICHAEL *enters.*

Michael, I've left you some fruit mince pies.

MICHAEL: Oh, thanks. Did something happen to one of your dogs?

ALISON: Oh, yes! It was terrible, Alfred's tail got trampled by one of the
donkeys. It was an accident, all concerned got quite a shock, donkey
included.

MICHAEL: Is Alfred alright?

ALISON: Oh, yes. Poor thing. He already had a ratty little tail and now
it's got a big bend in it. But he's been to the vet and they say he'll be
alright, and we've got him on the homeopathic medicine and he's
really perked up.

TOM: Which donkey was it?

ALISON: Don Quixote.

    ALISON *goes.*

MICHAEL: Those donkeys are a menace. The two old ones were sweet,
it was really sad when they died, but the two replacements are these
psychotic beasts that Alison rescued from a home for mistreated
animals. They see a human and they don't trust it and they try to
trample you. They seem to especially distrust me for some reason. I
don't know why the property even needed any more donkeys.

TOM: It's tradition. There are always two donkeys on the farm.

MICHAEL: Well, hopefully these ones get sick and Alison and Richard
will treat them with some homeopathic medicine and that will finish
them off. Their place is a mess. Garden's overgrown, chock-full of
snakes and rats, sometimes I think their garden will just grow over the
house. It's already happening to the back deck, their side has practi-
cally rotted through. It's dangerous.

    He stuffs a fruit mince pie into his mouth.

These are good. I find it such a bizarre choice of your parents', and
Alison and Richard, to move out here to the country, the main virtue
of which is being able to escape people, only to build a house that is
structurally and spatially intertwined with that of another family. At
least Sal and Ian had the good sense to build a separate house on the
other side of the property. Why not just build two houses? There's
enough room.

TOM: Us kids used to run back and forth through all the rooms, treat it all
as one big place that belonged to all of us.

MICHAEL: Yeah, well it would drive me up the wall. And it didn't last, I
mean no wonder they eventually divided the place completely in two.
Can't just wander back and forth anymore, thank God.

LILY *enters.*

LILY: Okay, the chairs are off the back lawn. You can mow.

MICHAEL: Great, I've been looking forward to that.

He goes out.

LILY: Do you think Mum and Dad will notice that we've gone to the effort? You know they're staying with us until after New Year's.

TOM: Well, it is their house.

LILY: I know. I think we just … need a bit of a break on our own, that's all.

TOM: You resent them coming here.

LILY: I do not.

TOM: You do!

LILY: Oh, come on, they're impossible to resent, they're so generous that if I were to resent them, what sort of person would that make me? They let us stay here on an absolute peppercorn rent. There's never been a more benevolent tyrant than Dad. He would never do anything that could possibly cause us to actually get angry with him, it's just that his goodness and his success exist as this kind of silent rebuke to us all.

TOM: The place looks different to how I remember it.

LILY: I guess it must.

TOM: I had the sense, walking through that door, this overwhelming sense that I was entering two houses. This house, the one that's here, and the one I've built in my memory of the place, which is all distorted. Huge. The ghost of a house. And of course all the cupboards and windows and door handles seem too low because I remember them being higher up.

Honestly, Lil, I think that no matter what you do, Dad at least will be compelled to fix something about the garden and Mum will talk about renovating the entire place.

LILY: Have you spoken to them since you got back?

TOM: No.

I talked to Mum just before I came home, I called her from Sweden. How're they doing?

LILY: Fine, I think. They've been staying down in town with Gran and Grandpa since they arrived from Sydney. Grandpa's worse, a lot worse, doesn't really recognise anyone anymore. I mean Gran, of course he recognises her, and Dad sometimes, but he probably won't know who you are.

The sound of a lawnmower chugging uncertainly into life.

Did Mum say anything to you about moving back here from Sydney?

TOM: About them moving back?

LILY: Yeah.

TOM: No, she didn't say anything. But it wasn't really that sort of conversation.

Do you think that they might?

LILY: Dad's been making noises.

TOM: Mum wouldn't want to move back here, not in a million years. She loves it in Sydney, they both do.

LILY: I thought so too, so I didn't take any notice the first couple of hints Dad dropped. But then he kept talking about Gran and Grandpa getting older, and how Alex and Hannah have the baby on the way, how it would be a shame not to be around.

TOM: But even if they did move back, it wouldn't be here, would it, not up here at the farm. They'd live in town, surely.

LILY: What, and just buy another house in town to go with this one and the one they have in Sydney?

TOM: I just don't think that Mum would want to move back here, Lil.

LILY: Maybe you're right, maybe I'm making it up.

TOM: I don't know. You have a way of being right about this sort of thing. How are you doing anyway? What's news?

LILY: We're good, Michael's got a really busy year next year, directing a couple of shows here and in Melbourne, which is great, so we'll be splitting our time between here and there, I think.

TOM: I did ask how you were, Lily, not about Michael.

LILY: I'm good. Just taking stock a bit, career-wise. I'm not quite sure yet what I'm interested in next. Just feeling a bit … in-between. Which is fine, it's good. I've got a couple of little gigs coming up but … I don't know if you know, my last show didn't go so well, I wasn't very happy with it myself, but … it's feeling like a long time since I worked on anything I thought was really good. I feel like … I dunno.

Slight pause.

TOM: Alison's looking older. More grey.

LILY: That's generally what happens, Tom, with time.
What will you do, now that you're back?

TOM: I might go for a walk up to the top paddock.

LILY: I meant with your life.

TOM: You think I should do something with my life?

LILY: Most people try to.

TOM: Well, I haven't made up my mind yet. Taking stock. See you soon.

He goes out the front door.

LILY *hovers near the fruit mince pies. She bites into one. She looks around the room, trying to figure out what else needs to be done. She sits down in a chair next to the table. The sound of a car arriving in the distance. The lawnmower sputters out.*

LILY: They're here.

She doesn't move. After a little while, we can hear voices, off.

JUDITH: [*off*] Hello, Michael!

MICHAEL: [*off*] Hi. Can I help you with that?

LILY *stands, folds up the little alfoil tray that the fruit mince pie had been in, and puts it in her pocket.*

JUDITH: [*off*] Oh, thanks. I know it looks a bit like we're coming for a month but I promise we're not, there's just a couple of things that I thought would look lovely in the dining room.

MICHAEL: [*off*] G'day, Patrick.

PATRICK: [*off*] Hi, Michael, how are you?

MICHAEL: [*off*] Yeah, not bad thanks.

PATRICK: [*off*] You've been mowing.

MICHAEL: [*off*] What? Oh, yeah, just my regular bit of regular weekend mowing.

JUDITH, *a small, sprightly woman with the manner of someone who has, with great determination and self-knowledge, throughout her life overcome a slight tendency towards hesitancy and self-doubt, enters.*

LILY: Hi, Mum.

JUDITH: Hello, dearie. Here we are!

LILY: Does anything else need to come out of the car?

JUDITH: I think that Michael and your father should have it covered. How're you going?

LILY: Fine.

JUDITH: Sorry we're a bit early.

LILY: No, you're not, you're right on time.

JUDITH: Whose car is that parked up the hill?

LILY: That's Tom's, he just beat you here.

JUDITH: Tom's here?

LILY: Yeah, he just went out for a walk, so should be back soon.

> PATRICK *enters, carrying some bags; a young-looking man around sixty, silver-haired, he's possessed of a great ease of manner that masks an inner steeliness and fierce intelligence.* MICHAEL *enters behind him, carrying a large amount of luggage.*

Hi, Dad!

PATRICK: Hello, Lilly-pilly.

LILY: You're growing a beard.

PATRICK: I'm on holiday. It's my customary holiday beard.

LILY: Aren't you meant to be permanently on holiday now that you're no longer a company man?

JUDITH: Well, you might have thought so, but actually he's working more than ever.

PATRICK: Not quite the punishing schedule of the last few years.

JUDITH: Almost.

PATRICK: Well, nothing but peace and quiet for the next two weeks.

JUDITH: I'm relieved we made it up the hill in that little old car.

PATRICK: Yes, it was quite sad, really. Mum gave us the keys, she's got them because Dad's not driving anymore. And the inside of the car had cobwebs all through it, strung up between the gearstick and the steering wheel, it had been that long since Dad was able to drive, and she doesn't seem to drive it at all.

LILY: I thought they were going to give it to the cousins.

PATRICK: Mum must have changed her mind. Anyway. It was a great relief when it started!

JUDITH: Oh, as we came up the road again to this place, it felt like it did the first time. That sense of discovering it for the first time. And it felt old, as well, ancient, this place that had wound itself into our bones. I don't think I've ever seen the hills looking so dry, though.

MICHAEL: Yeah, it's not been raining at all, even in winter they were barely green.

JUDITH: It was like that, do you remember, Pat, it was like that when we first came here. That fierce summer. Maybe it's a new beginning. I've had it with this year. It feels right, to be back here. Doesn't it? It feels right to me. Tom's here, Pat, Lily says that's his car on the hill.

PATRICK: Ah. When did he get here?

LILY: Just before you.

JUDITH: And we'll have Alex and Hannah up here tomorrow, the whole family! I can't remember the last time that we were all in the same place. Have you been baking, Lily?

LILY: No, these are from Ally.

JUDITH: Oh, let me have one. They're devastatingly good, Ally's fruit mince pies. Far surpass anything I was ever able to bake. Another of my failings. Mm. Yum.

> JUDITH *goes off into the next room, upstage right.*

MICHAEL: Actually, Patrick, I wanted to ask you—

LILY: Michael.

MICHAEL: Yeah? I just wanted to ask you about the sprinkler system, I think it needs a bit of work.

PATRICK: What's the problem?

MICHAEL: I dunno, it's just—the timer doesn't seem to be obeying the laws of physics, you set it for three o'clock and it turns on at seven.

PATRICK: Have you checked the pump, sometimes—

MICHAEL: Yeah, I had a look at it yesterday.

PATRICK: Well, I'll … see what I can see.

> JUDITH *comes back.*

JUDITH: That painting looks wonderful in there!

PATRICK: Probably it just needs a new timer, that one that's on it has been there for six years.

LILY: It's really not / that much of a problem.

JUDITH: Forgotten that we— / it's not one of ours, does it …

PATRICK: But I'll take a look. Well, where should we put our things?

LILY: You're in your room, it's all set up.

PATRICK: I'll / hoist these bags up there.

> PATRICK *goes out, with bags.*

JUDITH: Is anyone else having one of those fruit mince pies, / they're seriously good.

PATRICK: Save / one for me.

MICHAEL: No, not me.

JUDITH: Well. Here we are. Again. Sorry to land on you like this, I know you've both been busy as.

LILY: It's fine, Mum.

JUDITH: We heard wonderful things about your show, Michael, I'm sorry we couldn't make it down to Melbourne.

MICHAEL: Oh, don't worry about it. You can't see everything.

JUDITH: No, one can't. I've given up trying.

LILY: Michael, you should finish the mowing before Dad takes it on himself.

MICHAEL: What? Yeah, I'm nearly done.

> MICHAEL *goes out.*

JUDITH: Now tell me what I can do.

LILY: It's fine, Mum, it's all under control.

JUDITH: I made some salads in town, I brought them up, they're in one of these cool bags, it just saves time when there's so many of us. And I've got something for myself, I've got myself covered because I'm not eating meat anymore.

LILY: You're not?

JUDITH: No. When we were in Japan I didn't eat meat at all, except fish, and for whatever reason the habit's stuck. Except fish, I do eat fish because I think that ultimately, you know, humans do need some sort of—I don't think we're built to just eat vegetables—are you sure there's nothing I can do?

LILY: Positive.

JUDITH: Well, if there is anything, don't hesitate to put me to work. Darling?

LILY: I'm fine. It's good to have you both here. I'm sorry about the house, the garden, I know it looks like a mess.

JUDITH: I know how hard it is to keep up with it, I lived here for twenty-five years.

LILY: We've just been run off our feet, Michael especially.

> PATRICK *comes on, in very old gardening clothes—a faded blue shirt, trousers splotched with paint and with holes at the knees.*

Already, Dad?

PATRICK: Well, we stopped in at the nursery on our way up here so there's a bit of planting to be done. I thought I'd get in a couple of hours before it gets really hot. Where would I find the sunscreen?

LILY: In the—on the dresser in the bathroom.

PATRICK: Excellent.

He goes out into the corridor.

JUDITH: It is going to get hot today, isn't it?

LILY: Up to about thirty-seven, I think.

JUDITH: Sometimes I think he'd be perfectly content to just work in the garden. I think of him being in the middle of the rehearsal room, pulling all those strands of a production so delicately together, and probably all the while he's wishing he was in his garden building a wall or coaxing a tomato plant to grow over whatever bit of architecture he's created for it.

LILY: We used to live in terror of it, of disturbing his garden. When we'd play soccer on the back lawn and the ball would go into his veggie patch, it was like these storm clouds would descend on him.

Slight pause.

JUDITH: How's Tommy?

LILY: I only got to see him for a minute. He seemed fine.

JUDITH: I'm very glad he's come home. I think he got a bit lost over there.

MICHAEL *enters.*

LILY: Are you finished?

MICHAEL: Your dad offered to take over, and to be honest I don't think I was doing a very good job of it, it was quite uneven, I accidentally sliced right down to the dirt in a couple of patches, it's really not my strong suit, I usually more look after the … other parts of things. I like working in the vegetable garden, I like more physical things.

LILY: Well, that's excellent news, because you've been talking to me, haven't you, about doing the weeding in the front garden.

MICHAEL: What?

LILY: Haven't you.

MICHAEL: This is the bit where I'm meant to say, 'Oh, yes!', and hurry out, but we really didn't talk about the weeding of the front garden specifically. But I will go, I will do the weeding, because I love you.

He kisses LILY *on the cheek and goes out.*

LILY: I did ask him to, as it happens. I should help, I should pitch in. I really am sorry, Mum, that it's got this out of hand, I know it mustn't be nice to turn up to your house and see it … ramshackle.

JUDITH: Darling, don't mention it. How are you both, are you—?

LILY: We're great, we're really good. I'm just going to clean the pool and take a look at the front gate because those really are the last tasks on my list, so—

JUDITH: Right-o.

LILY: Help yourself to anything.

JUDITH: Yes, I might unpack. Get settled.

> LILY *goes out.* JUDITH *watches her for a little while.*

Hello, house.

Hello, old house.

I feel like you're rebuking me, house, for letting you go. I admit I'm not over you, but I have to say I don't miss you. Though you're so familiar. And familiarity is seductive.

I don't belong here anymore. The world's too different. I'm too different.

> TOM *comes in the front door.*

TOM: Hey, Mum.

JUDITH: Hi, dearie.

TOM: When did you arrive?

JUDITH: Not long ago. Did you go for a walk?

TOM: Yeah, just across the top paddock.

JUDITH: Did you drop in on Sal and Ian?

TOM: Nah.

JUDITH: I'm sure they'd like to see you.

> *Slight pause.*

Have you had one of these?

TOM: Yeah.

JUDITH: You're looking very thin.

Oh, we've had the strangest morning. We've been staying with Gran and Grandpa, we borrowed their second car to come up here. They asked after you, well Gran did. They'll be coming up here on Christmas Eve, you'll get to see them then.

Do you know I was your age when we first came here? No, younger. Back then there were none of the houses that are strewn all through the valley now. You couldn't even drive up this hill because there was no road, nothing. We parked at the foot of the hill and walked up, me and your dad and Alison and Richard and Sal and Ian, wading through the grass on this bare patch of land the six of us had cobbled together the deposit for. I would have been—yeah—your age. Golly. Time.

Your grandpa really isn't doing very well. He used to be such a tough man, I mean emotionally very reticent, that stiff upper lip thing. Your dad can be like that, every now and then I see a flash of it. It's terrible to see him … reduced. It's a horrible disease. Don't worry, you won't have to deal with it in my case, I fully intend to top myself before it gets that bad.

Although if it does get that bad and I haven't—which I fully intend to, I wouldn't want to leave it up to you—but if something happens then—just so we're clear, you switch me off. Sorry, not the right conversation, be quiet, Mum, sorry.

TOM: It's fine, Mum.

JUDITH: Sorry.

It is just such an awful disease. Worst way to go, I reckon. Robbed of yourself. I haven't even asked about your trip!

TOM: Oh, yeah it was good.

JUDITH: Where was your favourite place?

TOM: Hard to pick one.

JUDITH: Well, your top three then.

TOM: Paris was pretty amazing. I knew some people there, I think that helped. And my terrible French, I speak it very badly, but it helped just to have a bit, you know.

I don't know, they're just the same places that anyone's been, Mum, I don't think I made any startling discoveries.

JUDITH: No, but *you* haven't been there before. I'm interested.

TOM: I don't know.

To be honest it's a bit of a blur.

There was one week. In Scotland. I went right up north, this area near the North Sea. Lakes and mountains. Water so still and cold and clear. I was on my own, I'd go walking most of the day, just trudging along the lakeside, the water stretching around me in every direction. It was very peaceful. I think it might have been my favourite place.

JUDITH: It was so strange having you away, so suddenly. Out in the world. You were gone before we were home from Japan, it felt like we might have passed somewhere, high up in the air. No warning that you were going. That must have been exciting, just … spur of the moment. Going.

TOM: Yeah.

I spent all the money that your mum left to me, I know she wanted me to put it towards something more substantial, but …

JUDITH: That's alright. It's important to see the world.

TOM: There's nothing left.

JUDITH: Oh, don't worry, darling. It's so nice to see you. When I spoke to you from Japan. Before you left. And then when you called from Sweden—

TOM: Yeah, Mum—

JUDITH: I … I'm glad you came home.

TOM: Yeah. Home again, home again.

JUDITH: You stay here as long as you need, Lily and Michael can—

TOM: Yeah, I'm going to stay for a little while, it'll be nice.

JUDITH: Great.

TOM: Lily says you're moving back here.

JUDITH: Does she?

TOM: That Dad's been dropping hints. I thought you were happy in Sydney.

JUDITH: I am. We are.

TOM: Lily and Michael would get a shock, they're onto a good thing here.

JUDITH: They look after the place, it works well for us.

TOM: I'm just stirring, Mum.

JUDITH: Yairs.

TOM: Would you keep the place in Sydney, Mum, if you move back?

JUDITH: Tom, I've not said we're moving, it's not on the cards.

TOM: Oh. Then I was thinking—hoping, really, that I could, when I get back to Sydney, that I could stay with you and Dad.

JUDITH: Of course you can.

TOM: I don't have anywhere else. I'm not sure when I'll get back.

JUDITH: Just let us know, darling.

TOM: I mean I might sort something out, but just in case.

JUDITH: Sure.

   I need to get unpacked.

   I'll be back down in a minute.

   JUDITH *goes off.* LILY *comes on,* MICHAEL *chasing her.*

MICHAEL: Lily, have you asked your dad?

LILY: Ssh!

MICHAEL: Why won't you ask, there was the perfect moment!

LILY: I said I would, and I will!

TOM: Ask what?

LILY: Never mind.

   She goes off.

MICHAEL: You got published.

TOM: What?

MICHAEL: I read a poem of yours. In a reputable journal, Tom. I kind of surprised myself by buying it. I don't usually read those journals, it's more Lily's sort of thing. I didn't know you wrote poems.

TOM: Surprise.

MICHAEL: The family trade has got you after all.

TOM: I don't think I'd go as far as that, Michael.

MICHAEL: Your mum was a poet, before theatre got her.

TOM: I wrote one poem, Michael, a not very good one.

MICHAEL: You published one, you mean, you must have written others. Did you tell anyone it had been published?

TOM: It's not important.

MICHAEL: You must be at least a little proud of it if you submitted it for publication. Seriously, Tom, take some credit, people who are end-lessly self-effacing are eventually very dull to talk to.

TOM: I didn't submit it, Max did, without me knowing.

MICHAEL: Things didn't end too well between the two of you, did they?

TOM: No, they didn't. But then, what's ending well? That seems like a contradiction in terms to me.

MICHAEL: What happened?

TOM: Oh, let's not go into it. It's not a particularly edifying story.

   LILY *comes back on.*

MICHAEL: It's really easy, you just go up to your dad, and say, 'Hey, Dad, I just had something that I wanted to run by you …'

LILY: Michael, I'll handle it my own way.

MICHAEL: I just find your reluctance so strange!

They both go off. PATRICK *comes on from another direction, calling.*

PATRICK: Jude! Judith! Oh! Tommy.

TOM: Hi, Dad.

PATRICK: How good to have you here. Very glad that you could make it back.

They hug.

TOM: Well, it's not like I was especially busy anywhere else.

PATRICK: Did you have a good trip?

TOM: Yeah.

PATRICK: We'll have to see your photos at some point.

TOM: I lost my camera while I was over there. Well, I threw a lot of my things away, actually. How was Japan?

PATRICK: Quite wonderful. An extraordinary place. We travelled the whole time with an old friend of mine, did you ever meet Yoshika?

TOM: Name's familiar.

PATRICK: We collaborated on a project with her company, maybe twenty years ago, and she very occasionally guides small numbers of people on a sort of small cultural tour of Japan. And we were her only guests on this occasion so it was a really fantastic way of seeing a number of things that otherwise I think we wouldn't have been able to see. I'm just looking for your mother, we picked up some things at the nursery on the way up here, and they've been left in what's probably a very sensible spot and I can't find them.

TOM: She just went upstairs, but I'll go and check in the car if you like.

PATRICK: Thank you. And if you want to do some planting, Tommy, most of the seedlings are for the back garden, so get stuck in and I'll meet you out there, if you like.

TOM: Sure.

TOM *goes out the front door.*

PATRICK: Jude?

JUDITH *comes in through from the corridor.*

JUDITH: Yes, I'm here.

PATRICK: Do you know what happened to those plants we picked up at the nursery?

JUDITH: Oh. I left them in that polystyrene, um, container by the woodshed.

PATRICK: Of course.

JUDITH: There's a distinct smell of dead rat coming from the attic.

PATRICK: Yes, I noticed that. It's not in the attic, unfortunately, it's in the roof. Trying to crawl outside for water but carked it before it got there.

JUDITH: I checked the baits, we need to lay some more.

PATRICK: Yes. Things have been allowed to slide.

JUDITH: Cleaning up pieces of dead rat is one of the things I don't miss about this place.

PATRICK: I've always felt it was one of the highlights.

JUDITH: You have not. I do miss this place though. I tell myself that I don't, but I do.

PATRICK: Yes.

JUDITH: I thought of it like a prison for a while.

PATRICK: Really?

JUDITH: A beautiful prison.

PATRICK: Oh, I never would have thought you were trapped here. Against your will.

JUDITH: I brought up three small children, much of that without a driver's licence, or a car.

PATRICK: With help.

JUDITH: With great help. But you were away, often, and they were busy children. I would sit here at this table in the dark in the bare hours between when they would sleep and wake and I'd work, writing… what? Delirious stuff. I was so tired I can hardly remember. And I had no way of getting off the property and only Alison and Richard or Sal and Ian to talk to. It was madness. What if something had happened to them and I had to drive to the hospital? I wouldn't have been able to.

PATRICK: But you got it. The licence.

JUDITH: Eventually.

PATRICK: You got it.

JUDITH: It was a great failing I didn't get it sooner.

Pause.

I'm worried about Tom.

PATRICK: He's alright. He's here with his family.

JUDITH: He didn't want to be.

PATRICK: Well, he's here, so he must have wanted to at least a little.

JUDITH: I pestered him to get him here. Just like I had to pester him to get his first job, that was months of pestering. I don't know how to talk to him, anymore. He hardly even meets my eyes. We used to have such good talks.

PATRICK: He's just a bit bruised from the split with Max. Learning what it is to be on his own again. He'll come good.

JUDITH: The split with Max wasn't exactly recent, darling. But yes, a big love.

Lily and Michael seem happy here.

PATRICK: They do.

Pause.

JUDITH: We'll all be back here again tomorrow. You, me. Our kids. Their lovely beloveds. We'll all be sitting around that big old table.

I know you're ready to come back here, Pat, but I'm not sure what it would mean for me. One's future leaves signposts in a language you don't know yet, it's hard to be sure they're not sending you back the way you came. I wasn't happy here, not by the end, it was … so small, so isolating. I forget that, with time, but it's still there, just at the edge of my sight. And I don't want to come back here if it means coming back to an old version of our lives that we've already lived. I don't want to step back into a prison, darling. However beautiful.

PATRICK: No. I don't want that either. I wouldn't ask you to.

You're right, I am ready. But if it's not what you want, then we won't. So it's your call, darling. Whatever you decide.

Pause.

JUDITH: I'll get lunch underway.

PATRICK: Do you want a hand?

JUDITH: No no, you keep working if you want to.

PATRICK: Alright.

JUDITH: I'm sure they're just outside the woodshed.

PATRICK: Right-o.

He goes out. LILY *comes on.*

JUDITH: Well. Here we are again. Again.

    JUDITH *is crying a little.*

LILY: Mum?

JUDITH: Oh, how silly of me. Very silly. I was thinking of the day that we first moved into this house, when we finally shifted out of the shed we'd been living in while we built it, and I was thinking of you and Alex stepping up into your new house and how Alison and Richard were here, and their girls, and how all that's gone now, utterly gone. Time is so stealthy, so ruthless. Suddenly we're old. I never expected it.

LILY: Yes, it's probably time we put you on the scrap heap.

    JUDITH *laughs.*

JUDITH: Yes, washed up. Our best work behind us. Bring in the new victims.

    I've not been working very much, can't seem to, no-one's interested. I'm not even sure if I am. You think there'll be time for everything, but it's not true. Don't wait. I was going to make lunch but I don't feel hungry anymore. I'll go for my walk. That'll put me right.

    JUDITH *goes. After a little while,* MICHAEL *enters.*

MICHAEL: Lily? Did you ask them?

LILY: I'll ask them tomorrow.

END OF ACT ONE

ACT TWO: CHRISTMAS EVE

Late afternoon, drifting on into evening.

ALEX, a self-contained but energetic man in his early thirties, is in the kitchen, looking at his phone. HANNAH *is sitting on one of the couches, flicking through a magazine and sipping from a glass of mineral water. A highly perceptive person, she is nevertheless instinctively circumspect in her relationships with others. She's eight months pregnant.*

The house is still, silent, it's a warm afternoon melting into evening, and throughout the Act people come and go with an unwound air, often finding a quiet spot and reading, or getting themselves a snack from the fridge.

Silence for a little while, then HANNAH *puts down her magazine and looks around.*

HANNAH: How long has it been?

ALEX: Hm?

HANNAH: How long since we got here?

ALEX: I think, yeah, about an hour and a half.

HANNAH: Still no sign of anyone.

One of the things I love about this place is that no-one ever worries if someone's not on time. You could arrive here and wait, and sooner or later someone would show up. If someone died up here the body would have hardly any time to decompose before someone discovered it.

That was someone's car perched on the hill but I didn't recognise it.

ALEX: Hire car.

HANNAH: What?

ALEX: It was a hire car, I think it will have been Tom's.

HANNAH: I didn't know he was coming back this year.

ALEX: It's hard to keep track.

HANNAH: Why don't you talk to Tom more?

ALEX: What do you mean?

HANNAH: Well, he's your brother but you just don't seem to talk to each other so much, you never have. Months go by and you don't hear from him, he doesn't hear from us.

ALEX: You don't have to be talking every second day to be—

HANNAH: I know.

ALEX: But you're right. I don't know, he's a lot younger than Lil and I, so I guess when we were younger we didn't have that much to talk about really and the habit stuck. He would have been—what, eleven?—when I moved out of home. And then he went to Sydney with Mum and Dad. But then Tom's hard to pin down. No-one speaks that much to him, really, except Mum.

HANNAH: It's a shame.

ALEX: Yeah, it is.

How are you going over there?

HANNAH: Fine. They reckon it's going to get past forty degrees later in the week, and I'm not looking forward to that. With all this extra blood in me I might actually boil.

ALEX: That'd be something.

HANNAH: Yes, that would be a sight.

ALEX: What are you reading?

HANNAH: One of your mum's magazines. It's telling me that I can do incredible things with discarded materials.

What do you think will happen to this place when Lily and Michael move out? Would your mum and dad get tenants in again?

ALEX: I don't think so. That one set of tenants were the only ones they've had here. They were kind of a hard-luck case, they had this—things went wrong. I don't think they'll be keen to repeat the experience.

HANNAH: Do you know how much Lily and Michael pay in rent?

ALEX: You know, I've never been able to pin that down.

HANNAH: It's rude of me to ask. It's not like your parents haven't helped us out in the past.

ALEX: They offered, I didn't ask.

HANNAH: I know.

Pause.

But Lily and Michael won't stay here forever. What happens then?

ALEX: I think there's a slightly romantic idea that Mum and Dad might move back one day, but I can't see it happening, I don't really see that it's practical.

HANNAH: It'll just stay empty, then.

ALEX: Yeah, I suppose.

HANNAH: A whole empty house. Can you imagine what my dad would say about that? But I guess it makes sense. I can't imagine them selling the place. They built it.

ALEX: Yeah. They sure did.

HANNAH: And wouldn't it be all tied up with the other families they bought the land with anyway? It's not like your parents own a discrete block of land, it's a commune. It was.

ALEX: Commune. It was a hobby farm.

HANNAH: You're the one who first described it as a commune.

ALEX: Jokingly.

HANNAH: So what was it then? In earnest.

ALEX: Why are you so interested? You know all this.

HANNAH: I don't, not properly. If you had to take a course in becoming part of this family, then nearly everything about this place would be assumed knowledge. You never really talk about it.

ALEX: Okay then. In earnest. Three couples, all friends, bought the land together—for an absolute song—but hey, it was the seventies. And they helped each other build their houses. And we all lived here together. One big family, in a way. But time rolls on. It's all subdivided these days.

HANNAH: Do you remember it getting built? This place?

ALEX: Vaguely. I don't know, I was so young I can't tell if they're my memories or if I think I remember it because I've been told about it so much. But if you stand up there outside the old shed—

HANNAH: Which old shed? There are a few.

ALEX: The blue one, the shed we lived in for the first two years of my life—you can look down on this house. I remember the building site from that angle, looking down on it. I kind of remember it being half-completed and then suddenly, one morning, there it was. Like it just dreamed itself up.

Slight pause.

I wouldn't have thought they'd ever sell it, they love it too much.

HANNAH: And their children love it.

ALEX: Yeah. But then people change. What they need are changes. Mum and Dad never expected to move away from here, but they did. I don't think any of us kids will ever live here permanently so … who knows? If it were just going to be empty they might think about selling it, I guess.

HANNAH: Would you be sad if they sold it?

ALEX: Yeah, of course. Of course I'd be sad, I love it. We all do. It's our childhood. But we're not children anymore.

Pause.

HANNAH: It's so quiet. It could almost be inside a theatre.

ALEX: Yeah, just replace the birds with the gentle buzz of hearing aids and we'd be there.

JUDITH *enters, carrying a book.*

JUDITH: Hello hello.

ALEX: Hi, Mum.

JUDITH: Hi, darling. Have you been here long?

HANNAH: Not long.

JUDITH: I was doing my yoga and I got to the end and fell asleep. Is anyone else about?

ALEX: Haven't seen anyone.

JUDITH: Oh. Well, I suppose they'll drift in at some point. I'll put the kettle on.

ALEX: But it's so hot.

JUDITH: I'm not sure that we're worrying about dinner, just pick from whatever's there.

ALEX: Did you have a good flight over?

JUDITH: Yes, uneventful.

Gran and Grandpa are joining us up here tonight. I offered to go into town to pick them up but your gran insisted she'd manage. I don't like to think of her driving up that hill, but what can you do? How're you going, Hannah?

HANNAH: Oh, good. Happy to be getting close to the final countdown.

JUDITH: Alex was nearly two weeks overdue. We got in the Land Rover and drove over and over the rocky patch in the front paddock to try to get things started. To no avail. He came when he was good and ready. Tom was born in the full heat of January, so I know what you're going through. I'd sit there on that same couch at night when I had a minute to myself.

HANNAH: He's been moving around a fair bit, do you want to have a feel?

JUDITH: Yes please.

JUDITH *puts her hand on* HANNAH's *belly.*

HANNAH: Got a kick for Gran?

JUDITH *laughs a little uncertainly at this title, not used to it.*

JUDITH: Hello, little creature.

HANNAH: He really was— / oh!

JUDITH: Oh! Hello there. That was emphatic.

HANNAH: He's fierce. Keen to meet you, I guess.

JUDITH: Yes. Oh, you've been reading that. I've discovered relatively late in life that I have a clandestine and perhaps slightly shameful enthusiasm about home decoration. Or homes in general. It's taken ten years of work but the house in Sydney is finally the way we want it. It's looking beautiful now the renovation's finished. Plenty of room. It's a shame you aren't all closer to us to make use of it.

HANNAH: Yes.

It's a good magazine.

JUDITH: Yes, cheap thrills. Until you get persuaded to buy something from it.

Pat's been throwing himself at the garden. He's probably out there now, somewhere, some hidden corner. Tom's here as well, he's come home, I don't know if you know.

ALEX: I guessed the car must have been his.

PATRICK *enters.* JUDITH *continues to speak, though not addressing him specifically.*

JUDITH: I was trying to write all morning but nothing, nothing. Not so unusual.

JUDITH *settles down on one of the couches and reads her book.*

PATRICK: Hello hello.

JUDITH: Not so unusual really.

ALEX: Hi, Dad. Been in the garden?

PATRICK: Trying to reclaim the chook shed.

ALEX: That's a bit of a job.

PATRICK: I never really completed it to my satisfaction while we lived here, and now it's been idle so long that the bracken is encroaching. Hi, Hannah.

HANNAH: Hi, Patrick, good to see you, welcome home.

PATRICK: Yes, good to be back. How's the future coming along?

HANNAH: Pretty rowdy, but the right way up at least.

PATRICK: Anyone else about?

ALEX: No.

PATRICK: Ah well, they'll drift in. I haven't seen Michael all day though.

JUDITH: No, I haven't either. Dodging being put to work in the garden.

PATRICK: Well, I think it's lunchtime. Did you happen to bring a paper up with you?

ALEX: Yeah.

He goes and gets the newspaper from his bag and hands it to PATRICK, *then turns his attention back to his phone.*

PATRICK: Waiting for a call?

ALEX: The job I went for at the Festival. Second interview was nearly two weeks ago, so I should be hearing about it any minute and I have this irrational expectation they'll call today. They said they would before the New Year.

He taps away at his phone.

There's hardly any reception up here though.

HANNAH: I usually have some luck if I stand out on the road.

ALEX *wanders out the front door as* ALISON *and* TOM *wander in. They're both carrying some large pieces of discarded cardboard that have been drawn all over by children.*

ALEX: Hi, Ali.

ALISON: Hello, dear.

ALEX: You're home!

TOM: Yes, back again.

ALEX: I just have to—

TOM: Sure.

ALEX *goes out.*

ALISON: Well, we're no closer to solving the mystery.

TOM: No.

ALISON: Perhaps you and our girls wrote a rulebook, now lost to humanity, that might have unlocked these.

TOM: I just can't make any sense of them. They must have made sense at one point, but maybe only to a kid's brain. I can hardly even read the writing.

ALISON: Well, I'll leave them with you. Maybe the next thing I work on will be a tribute to these board games, a kind of artistic re-creation. I've got an exhibition coming up in June, I could change tack and start working on some paintings inspired by these. They could call the exhibition 'Lost Arts of the Hills'. I should keep moving. Lots to do before tomorrow. See you later.

ALISON *goes out the front door.*

JUDITH: See you, Ally.

PATRICK: I was sure we brought a jar of pickles up with us. Jude? Did we bring those pickles?

JUDITH: I thought so. What have you got there, Tommy?

TOM: Board games. I made them when I was little.

JUDITH: Oh, how wonderful. Ally's kept them all these years.

TOM: Yeah. Hi, Hannah.

HANNAH: Hi, Tom.

TOM: Look at you.

HANNAH: I know, there's been some progress since you went away.

TOM: Sure has.

LILY *comes on through the front door, carrying a cardboard box filled with bottles of wine.*

LILY: Hi, everyone.

HANNAH: Everyone's coming out of the woodwork now.

TOM: Where have you been?

LILY: Picking up the wine for tomorrow. We've got a friend who works for one of the wineries down the road, so I went to take delivery of our Christmas order. There's more boxes in the car if anyone wants to bring some in. Has anyone seen Michael?

HANNAH: No.

TOM: No.

PATRICK: I have not.

LILY: I thought he must have been helping you, Dad. He said he was going to come with me. He's disappeared off the face of the earth. I'll just put these in the laundry.

LILY *goes off through the corridor.*

TOM: I'll get the rest.

TOM *goes out the front door.*

Alex!

ALEX: [*off*] What?

TOM: Can you help?

ALEX: [*off*] Just a minute, I had two bars a second ago.

HANNAH: Is it nice being back?

PATRICK: It is. Since I finished up at the company it's been on my mind in a way it hasn't been for years. All the things we never quite finished.

LILY *enters from the corridor.*

HANNAH: You've been attacking the garden nonstop, Judith said.

PATRICK: Yes. Plans are afoot. I think maybe we'll re-terrace the front garden, and we need to take down the fence that's around the yard at the moment and replace it. I was thinking as well, Jude, of a bit of a deck on that side of the house, to get the view of the hills.

JUDITH: I would suggest one thing at a time, but it's never been advice that stuck.

PATRICK: Well, one can't help getting a little carried away.

JUDITH: I know.

PATRICK: We need to rip up that old brick pathway that's there at the moment at the very least. But that's all … if I can just get the garden into decent shape while I'm here that would feel perfectly satisfying.

HANNAH: I still can't believe that you built this whole place yourselves. This house, the whole property.

PATRICK: Well, we hired some people to do the brickwork on the inside of the chimney.

JUDITH: It was the times. There was a whole movement, you know, to live more simply, more sustainably, with nature. Oh, and we were very passionate about it. That was the principle with this place, to be entirely self-sufficient, and we came close to it, for some years. I know we ended up working as artists and the property fell by the wayside, but really sustainability was, we thought, an equal passion. But I think, ultimately, that we underestimated ourselves. As people we were built to do certain things and we thought that we could ignore the pull of art, but really we couldn't. Sustainability and theatre fought it out, and theatre won.

PATRICK: It was a dream we were building, I suppose.

ALEX *comes in through the front door.*

But, really, it didn't seem so fanciful at the time. I mean we hear the arguments about climate change now, in the past ten, twenty years, and we feel like they're new, but actually people have been saying it for a very long time, a depressingly long time, until suddenly—here we are at this tipping point. In our day, really, it was more about pollutants and population pressure. And rejecting the strangely enduring popular fallacy that we can indefinitely consume more than the planet's able to provide. But still, it was there, creeping closer and closer into sight.

JUDITH: We really, truly thought that you could change the world through love. It sounds so daft now, but those were the times. We did believe it. And I'm not ashamed to have believed it, it's a beautiful thing to have believed.

TOM *comes on, carrying a box of wine.*

PATRICK: And this place was born from that. An attempt, however unsuccessful, however compromised it ended up being, it was an attempt to live better with nature. To make a home for our children and the children of our friends that we could be proud of. Of course the wind generator we bought stayed in the shed until it was rusted and unusable, when we were starting we were too poor to really do it properly, and time, and the changes time brings, meant that the community we ended up with wasn't the one we first envisaged, but that's alright. We did try. With some measure of success, I think. To make that place. It is, still, a dream. Maybe it's our life's work, this place, you kids. More than anything else.

JUDITH: Hopefully it's something we can pass on to you.

PATRICK: When I think of what the future might be on our poor little planet ... it seems to me that there's a very animal panic somewhere in humanity's deep brain, the reptile part of our collective unconscious, that knows that things are going to get much more ugly before they get better. If they get better again.

The sound of someone playing a recorder. It's a version of 'Twinkle, Twinkle, Little Star' with some slight flourishes.

JUDITH: What's that?

LILY: Alison. She's teaching herself how to play the recorder. You can hear her better from our room. I love to listen to her playing. It sounds like something from the past.

JUDITH: It's getting late.

Look at you all. My kids. I've got you all in the same place. Up here at our beautiful home. We're so lucky.

TOM: Except that we're all unemployed apart from you and Dad.

LILY: And Hannah.

TOM: What are you doing at the moment, Hannah?

HANNAH: I'm working for the opera company, part-time, in philanthropy. Not exactly my usual line, but it looks like I'll be able to structure it around the baby and it makes use of my skill set. It's going well.

TOM: But still, Alex is in between jobs, unless he becomes the—what? Associate Producer at the Festival?

ALEX: Senior Producer.

TOM: Right, sorry, and that wouldn't start until …

ALEX: March.

TOM: So, Alex is between jobs, Lily's got no work, Michael's got a good year next year but it's been a long time coming. And the less said about me, the better.

LILY: I think it's more a case of the less you say, the better, Tom.

PATRICK: It's a fallow period. The wheel turns.

TOM: Yes, it spins around and around in the air, never touching the ground.

LILY: Maybe we should treat this Christmas like an unemployment retreat.

ALEX: Unemployment Farm.

TOM: Yes, that's brilliant!

HANNAH: What shall we do today on Unemployment Farm?

ALEX: I think most of what we'll be doing is eating, drinking, and sleeping. We can't be that worried, can we?

LILY: Oh, we laugh about it but it's such a totally shithouse feeling.

TOM: No prospects whatsoever.

ALEX: Have you seen me checking my phone? I know they're not going to call but I keep checking. Somehow I never quite envisioned being potentially unemployed at the same time as having a newborn baby. I'm really not sure what we'll do if I don't get it.

HANNAH: We'll figure it out.

JUDITH: Maybe we didn't … stress enough that there were other ways of living a life that can be free from the very particular heartbreak that tends to come with theatre. Because I think that more often than not, no matter who you are, or how good, or how successful, it is a life of endless reaching, and endless falling short. Relentless struggle. And stupid, pigheaded obsession. I mean I've had my time. Theatre's a young person's game, by and large. But I can't help it. I can't stop writing as much as stop breathing. It's the obsession that's the thing, in the end. The possibility that it could suddenly all go right and you end up at art. True art. That clean thing. But that's rare, I think most people never get to experience it, the doing of it.

Maybe once or twice. But it's the thing that keeps us coming back, that keeps us locked in it. That possibility. Hope. Hope, I guess, in the end. It's an optimist's profession, however cynical one might be on any given day. Which is why it seems so cruel when it all goes wrong, because it seems like a punishment of hope.

ALEX: Well, it's a bit late to hear all this now.

LILY: After you suckered us into it.

PATRICK: I feel like we were always very balanced in the options we presented.

JUDITH: If any of you were to turn around tomorrow and wanted to do something else, I'd say go for it.

LILY: Thanks, Mum, very encouraging.

JUDITH: I only meant that I'd support you.

TOM: Can we not talk about the theatre?

LILY: What do you want to talk about?

TOM: I don't know, anything else. I wish one of us were an engineer, or a metallurgist, then at least out of politeness we'd have to make a conversational gambit with something other than stupid, boring theatre.

ALEX: Maybe you should become an engineer, Tom, can they transfer your credit points from either of your abandoned degrees?

TOM: I should look into that.

ALEX: You should finish them, Tom, you must be close. It would stand you in really good stead.

TOM: Yeah, I know.

LILY: What's everyone getting everyone else for Christmas?

JUDITH: Your father's getting me a rather beautiful vase.

PATRICK: Am I?

JUDITH: You are. It's beautiful.

PATRICK: That was thoughtful of me. I wonder what I'm getting.

JUDITH: You'll find out on the day.

ALEX: Well, we all know who the worst present is going to come from.

TOM: I know, I know, but I feel like it's kind of become a tradition: 'And what shit present did Tom get for us all this year?' I do have vague notions of one day really pulling out all the stops and getting something for everyone that puts all the other presents to shame, but I never do it.

LILY: Tom, Dad just gives us money, I'm pretty sure more effort goes into picking out whatever discounted book or CD we inevitably get from you.

TOM: Money's a great gift, it's exactly what we all need! I'm relying on Dad's trusty hundred-dollar Christmas cheque!

JUDITH: You know, if we ditched that old dresser, that would be a beautiful spot to hang something, against that wall.

And a fountain, in the garden, that you could see through that window.

LILY: A fountain? With the rainfall we get up here?

JUDITH: It would be beautiful.

LILY: Dad? A fountain?

PATRICK: I'm not against the principle of a fountain.

LILY: Well. You two have come a long way.

JUDITH: And we're getting ahead of ourselves. The only urgent thing is the bloody laundry. If we were going to sell the place that would be the thing that absolutely needed to get fixed.

Slight pause.

PATRICK: Has anyone seen Michael anywhere? Lilly-pilly, do you—?

LILY: No, I don't know where he is.

PATRICK: I was going to ask for his help with putting in some new fencing around the chook shed.

ALEX: I'll help, Dad.

PATRICK: You just got here, relax!

ALEX: No, no. Put me to work, it'll keep me from being distracted by a phone call that isn't going to arrive.

PATRICK: Alright. Well, let's get to it while we've still got light.

ALEX: Sure.

JUDITH: Keep an eye out for your folks, Pat, they should be arriving soon.

ALEX *and* PATRICK *go out the front door.*

LILY: Where are they staying tonight, Mum?

JUDITH: In our room, Pat and I will shift to the pool house for tonight. The futon's still in there, isn't it?

LILY: Yes, but we can—

JUDITH: No no, it's fine, I've already thought it through, just need to get it all set up.

LILY: Sorry, I hadn't quite caught up that they were coming this evening and—

JUDITH: It's fine, darling, I'd had it all planned.

JUDITH *goes out through the corridor.*

LILY: You'd never know that they hadn't lived here for more than ten years.

I feel so lazy watching Dad work in the garden, I can't relax while he's working.

I might go and see if they need a hand.

LILY *goes out the front door.*

HANNAH: It's nice to see your dad and Alex working together. I've always loved this place. Maybe that comes as a surprise to you, but it's true. Ever since I first came here. There's a kind of feeling to it, isn't there? I've always had a sense that this is a safe place, you know. And I don't mean in a hippy-dippy way, like an aura or something, it's just how I've always felt when we've come here. You know I grew up not far from here, very close in fact, but worlds apart. My family would never talk about art or theatre or … politics. And we were just a couple of towns over. Driving up here from the city feels familiar and strange all at once. There's a particular turn I always half-expect to take but we don't, we're on our way here, not home.

TOM: I think there's a point where time and place become more or less the same thing. You're driving back through time, through the person you used to be, as much as you're driving along a road towards home.

HANNAH: Well, it's a nice surprise for us to see you here, Tom, last we heard you were still going to be overseas.

TOM: It was a last-minute decision. I really thought of not coming this year. As a statement, you know. 'I am my own person in the world, I don't need to come home.' But then I thought it doesn't matter where you go, you're still the same person, you're still stuck with yourself, might as well come home. Come back.

HANNAH: How long will you stay? Maybe you'll be here when the baby arrives.

TOM: Yeah, maybe.

HANNAH: It'll be nice to have people around.

Slight pause.

I had a dream the other night that I gave birth but there were no other people left anywhere on the entire planet.

JUDITH *comes on through the corridor.*

This heat. I'm surprised there haven't been fires yet this year. Alex looks like he's struggling a little. He's not wearing a hat.

> HANNAH *picks up a hat from a pile of them sitting near the front door and goes out the front.*

Al? Hat!

> *She goes off towards the garden.*

TOM: I don't think you should move back here, Mum.
I think that it would be a mistake.

> *Perhaps the sound of a car arriving, distant hellos.*

JUDITH: That'll be your dad's folks.

> JUDITH *goes out the front door.* MICHAEL *enters, carrying a basket of plums and wearing a floppy, white, wide-brimmed hat that's too small for his head.*

MICHAEL: Where was everyone?

TOM: What?

MICHAEL: Weren't we all meant to be picking the fruit together?

TOM: I don't think so.

MICHAEL: I thought some kind of activity had been planned.
I was in the orchard, I picked all these plums.
Bloody hell.
Lily?

> *He goes back out the front door.* ALEX *comes on.*

ALEX: Tom, have Mum and Dad said anything to you about moving back here?

TOM: No, nothing concrete. Why?

ALEX: Something's going on. Dad's been repairing things that he's left untouched for ten years. And did you hear what Mum said before about fixing the laundry and selling the place?

TOM: Yeah, but she's also talking about a fountain.

ALEX: That's true. What would you think, Tom, if the place got sold?

TOM: I don't think it's our choice.

ALEX: Well, of course not, but if Mum and Dad aren't moving back and they're talking about selling the place … maybe that could be a good thing.

LILY, MARY, DONALD, JUDITH, HANNAH and PATRICK start to come on—these lines can occur along the back wall or offstage and can overlap; it should feel full, the bubbling of conversation, of life.

PATRICK: This way, Mum.

MARY: It's a long time since we've been here, isn't it, Don?

JUDITH: You alright, Don?

DONALD: Oh, another kind and helpful person.

JUDITH: How was the drive?

DONALD: Yes, in the car.

HANNAH: I like your hat, Don, very stylish.

MARY: Those sheep on the hill wouldn't get out of my way, I had to bip them with my horn.

PATRICK: Yes, they're a stubborn breed.

LILY comes on through the front door, sees ALEX and TOM.

LILY: Christmas!

DONALD, MARY, JUDITH, HANNAH and PATRICK come in through the front door.

The following dialogue can overlap a lot:

MARY: Where are we? Hello Tom, hello Alex.

PATRICK: In the front room.

DONALD: Hello.

JUDITH: Alright with that step?

DONALD: Yes.

LILY: Is there anything else in the car, Gran?

LILY goes out the front door.

MARY: No, no.

PATRICK: I'll take your bags through, Mum.

MICHAEL comes on from the laundry.

ALEX: Has anyone thought about how we're all going to fit in this house?

JUDITH: Yes, there's a plan, and it's just for one night.

MICHAEL: Lily?

MICHAEL goes back off. PATRICK exits through the corridor. LILY comes back on through the front door.

MARY: Look at this place!

DONALD: Thank you, very kind.

MARY: Look at you boys, give me a kiss.

TOM: Hi, Gran.

DONALD: Very good floors you have here. / Solid.

ALEX: Hi, Gran, was the drive up okay?

JUDITH: Yes, we're quite pleased with them.

MARY: Yes, fine.

DONALD: You've grown.

LILY: No. / Do you want to give me that, Gran?

DONALD: Hasn't she grown?

ALEX: I guess you're getting shunted to the pool house, Tom. Is my old sofa bed still in there?

DONALD: Must be easy to, easy to … yairs.

TOM: Yes.

ALEX: Actually, I think there's a whole lot of stuff I've stored here that I've forgotten about. What's out there?

ALEX *goes out the front door.*

LILY: Yes, there is, a lot, / it takes up a lot of space. I've told you about it, you can come and collect it any time.

HANNAH: Shall I take this upstairs?

JUDITH: Lily, I think I left the gate unlatched, would you mind checking? I don't want the sheep to get in.

MARY: Which way?

LILY: Yes, I'm onto it.

JUDITH: Through here, Mary.

JUDITH, DONALD *and* MARY *go out through the corridor.*

MARY: Here we go.

LILY: Yep.

TOM: Michael's looking for you.

LILY *goes out through the front door. As the family disperses throughout the house,* TOM *folds up the board games he made as a child and puts them in the bin.*

END OF ACT TWO

ACT THREE: CHRISTMAS DAY

Early afternoon.

There's been a Christmas lunch in the neighbouring dining room, and now the house's inhabitants are drifting somewhat. PATRICK *and* MARY, *a fit, disciplined woman in her early eighties, are packing some things away in the kitchen.*

PATRICK: Dad seems like he's doing well today.

MARY: Yes, today's quite good.

PATRICK: Still, even now it surprises me that whatever the course of this disease, the constant downward slope, he's still able to rise to an occasion.

MARY: Well, he rises as far as he can. It's like a lifebuoy rising through an ocean. Even if it floats all the way to the surface it's never going to get airborne, is it?

PATRICK: No.

MARY: But he likes having people around. He's always been a people person.

PATRICK: Just let us know when you want us to drive you back in to town.

MARY: I can still drive.

PATRICK: It's no trouble. Someone needs to go in to pick up Alex and Hannah's other car in any case.

MARY: Alright, thank you. I don't think we'll be much longer. He gets tired. It's very nice to have you home. And to be up here. I'm glad to get a look at the place again, it's been so many years.

PATRICK: Well, we're thinking of moving back here.

MARY: Are you? Why?

PATRICK: My full-time position's wound up, so I can pick and choose my projects a bit more now. If I need to go to Sydney they'll put me up. I'd like to be a bit closer to you and Dad. And with the baby on the way as well.

MARY: Don't you do anything on my account, dear.

PATRICK: I don't know if you've thought any more, Mum, about finding a more sustainable system to put in place with Dad.

MARY: Oh yes, I looked at the brochure you sent me.

I just don't know how he'd fare in a place like that.

PATRICK: These places, at least the ones I spoke to, mentioned that they often have a waiting period of eighteen months or more, so it's not necessarily about what the situation is like now, you do have to anticipate—

MARY: How can you anticipate?

PATRICK: Well, you can anticipate that things aren't going to get any better.

MARY: I know that, his brain's rotting, I know that, I know the grisly details.

PATRICK: I'm thinking more of you, Mum.

MARY: I'm thinking more of me as well. Loneliness makes one selfish. I've seen those places, my mother went into one, don't forget. There are some things I'm reluctant to have on my conscience.

PATRICK: Some of them are very good. You can afford it.

MARY: Yes, I could get the money, I could pay them.

PATRICK: Well yes, actually, that is the transaction, but it doesn't make it sordid.

MARY: It does to my mind. I'm not discounting it but it does seem sordid.

I know you're concerned, but we do manage pretty well, by and large. I know that he hasn't been well the last couple of times you've seen him, but it's not like that all the time, it's … some days are … fine, really fine.

TOM *and* DONALD *come on from the dining room.* DONALD *is in his eighties, quite hunched over. Once a fit man, years of decreasing activity have made him quite thin. He moves very slowly.*

DONALD: You're a helpful young person.

TOM: I do my best, Grandpa.

DONALD: Very kind of you to get the door for me. And you keep to a very helpful pace, as well, not very much … mm. Which is … good because I have something to lean on, which is most … reassuring.

TOM: Do you want to sit on the couch, Grandpa?

DONALD: Yes, that seems like a good spot.

TOM *helps* DONALD *down to the couch.*

I won't get back up, now.

TOM: You can have a snooze if you want.

DONALD: [*laughing*] I may well.

MARY: Are you alright, dear?

DONALD: This woman really is very tiresome, she keeps on at me. Yes, I'm three bags full.

> JUDITH, HANNAH, *and* LILY *come on from the dining room, carrying stacks of dirty plates, cutlery, baking dishes. Various people either clean them, dry them, put them away in cupboards, or put them in the dishwasher throughout the Act.*

HANNAH: I was looking on the news last night and they were saying that between now and New Year's that the fire danger is severe.

LILY: In which areas?

HANNAH: I don't know the names of all of them, it seems like pretty much everywhere.

JUDITH: There are fires in Victoria this year.

HANNAH: But south of the city was definitely mentioned, so we're on the list.

JUDITH: Well, I can't remember a drier summer.

LILY: We've been trying to reduce the fuel load in the pine forest but it's just such a massive job. Did they include today, Hannah?

HANNAH: No, I think there are some winds coming through later in the week that will make it worse.

JUDITH: It is strangely similar to the last time we had a fire here, when Alison lost her studio in the forest. We thought that we would save it, but the wind changed, and the fire wrapped around this little pine building filled with paints and oils and it basically exploded.

MARY: Shall we take a look at the garden, darling?

DONALD: If we must.

> TOM *helps* DONALD *up.*

MARY: Where have we left your hat?

PATRICK: They're just on the chair outside, Mum.

> DONALD *and* MARY *go out the front door.*

JUDITH: I've said it to Tom, but for your benefit, Lily, if my brain starts to go, put a pillow over my face.

LILY: I'm sure we'd find a gentler way of bumping you off, Mum.

HANNAH: We'd try to catch you by surprise.

>   JUDITH *gets the giggles.*

JUDITH: Well, catching me by surprise probably won't be hard when I'm in that state.

LILY: We'll drown you in the bath, that would be nice, wouldn't it?

JUDITH: Or just hand me over to a nursing home, they'll give me a nice rub down with kerosene.

>   *She sees* PATRICK*'s face.*

Sorry, darling.

>   ALISON *comes on through the front door.*

ALISON: Merry Christmas, Merry Christmas. I'm just passing through, like a swift reindeer. I just brought you some Christmas eggs because our chooks seemed to realise it was Christmas and all decided to lay eggs, a bit like Mary. We're calling all our chooks Mary this year.

LILY: Your shoes are wonderful, Ally.

>   DONALD *comes back on through the front door.*

ALISON: Yes, they're my Christmas clogs. Probably not the most suitable things for the climate, but they've become a tradition. I've got a basket of zucchinis up by the gate for you as well if some helpful person wanted to bring them down, we've got lucky with the zucchinis this year, we've got more than we can use.

PATRICK: I'll give you a hand, Ally. I wanted to take a look at your new chook set-up as well.

ALISON: Yes, it's a bit over the top but Richard's made some quite good innovations. I'll give you the tour. Merry Christmas!

>   *Whoever is nearby replies, 'Merry Christmas!'*

>   ALISON *and* PATRICK *go out the front door.*

JUDITH: You weren't interested in the garden, Don?

DONALD: No. I seem to be … displaced.

JUDITH: Do you want to sit down and I'll get you a cup of tea?

DONALD: Yes, that seems like a …

>   JUDITH *sits* DONALD *back down.* MICHAEL *comes on from the dining room.*

MICHAEL: One of my favourite things about this family is that no-one gives a shit about the cricket. If we were with my family the whole of the conversation would revolve around what would happen tomorrow on the Boxing Day test, and here, it hasn't come up once, it's brilliant.

HANNAH: I'm with you, Michael, I couldn't agree more.

LILY: What were you doing in there?

MICHAEL: I was finishing my lunch! There was so much left over and I didn't want to see it go to waste. Look, Hannah, I think I'm pregnant now as well. A Christmas baby.

>   MICHAEL *makes no move to assist with the washing up. He taps away at his iPhone.*

JUDITH: There's your dad and gran out in the garden. They were so sceptical of the life we said we wanted to live, but they still went guarantor when we bought this place. Then they'd dutifully come up here on weekends to help build the house. And, Don, you collected me from prison when I was arrested at the anti-war protests. You bailed me out.

DONALD: Did I?

JUDITH: Yes, you were at the time a little bit ashamed, but you did. Maybe more frustrated than ashamed.

HANNAH: I didn't know you were arrested, Judith.

JUDITH: Me and a lot of others. I was the smallest, most easily carried link in the human chain, that was my misfortune. You didn't see the police hauling off many fat protesters.

>   ALEX *comes in from the front door, putting his phone away.*

HANNAH: Darling, they're not going to call you on Christmas Day.

ALEX: I know, I know that logically but some weird part of my brain keeps suggesting that they might so I have to check.

JUDITH: Who's calling?

ALEX: I'm waiting to hear about that job.

JUDITH: Oh, of course.

ALEX: I actually feel like I'm in with a good chance, so … but the phone's going away, it's going away. What can I do?

HANNAH: There might still be some things in the dining room that need to be brought in.

MICHAEL: The police have caught someone trying to light a fire in a national park.

JUDITH: Well, if that was Christmas lunch, we've done it. Done for another year. A year in which I, for one, failed to get anything much significant done at all.

LILY: Except have two plays on, one of them in Korea, and you travelled to Japan.

JUDITH: Old plays, and insignificant productions.

HANNAH: This year has felt a bit like pushing shit up a hill and all I've found out is that the hill is bigger than I thought it was.

LILY: Well, I feel proud of what I've managed to do this year.

HANNAH: And Michael's having a lot of success.

JUDITH: Yes, it's wonderful, but forgive me, Michael, you're flavour of the month at the moment, but you'll be on the scrapheap soon enough. That's how it goes.

ALEX: I think that if a couple of things fall into place everyone's in line to have a really great year.

JUDITH: No-one has any attention span, you see.

MICHAEL *is still surfing the internet on his iPhone.*

MICHAEL: What's that?

ALEX: How is it that you get a signal here but I can't?

PATRICK *comes back on through the front door.*

PATRICK: Well, I think it's almost time for a bit of afternoon gardening. There's a particular patch of bracken I'd like to destroy, so something of a group effort to crush it down might be required.

LILY: I don't think I could move, Dad. Why do we always make so much food?

HANNAH: And the pace of celebrations doesn't let up, once Christmas is done we've got Boxing Day with my family, and then back up here for New Year's Eve, then it's your wedding anniversary almost immediately, which I think we should do something special for this time around.

LILY: Of course it is! What anniversary is it coming up?

PATRICK: Forty years.

HANNAH: You must have been young.

PATRICK: Well, I realised that once you were married, you were classified as independent as far as the government was concerned, and therefore eligible for all the benefits that accompanied being independent.

JUDITH: Our engagement rings cost five dollars, as I recall. Two people played mandolins as we left the church. Such were the times.

PATRICK: And our wedding was on the second of January, timed perfectly to ensure that we were eligible for a full twelve months government assistance.

ALEX: On top of your free university education.

PATRICK: This is true. And so, having qualified for various bits and pieces of government assistance, we saved assiduously. The place we rented was ten bucks a week, and another ten covered transport and groceries. And having saved for a while, we travelled around Europe for seven months on the benefits of Gough Whitlam's Australia.

JUDITH: We worked while we were there.

PATRICK: A bit. For a month. But I think it's fair to say that a child born in Australia today couldn't expect such a start in life.

ALEX: Dad, I think it's safe to say that a child born, oh, thirty-two years ago couldn't expect it.

PATRICK: We were a fortunate generation, by and large, it's true.

JUDITH: Those of us who didn't get packed off to fight in Vietnam. That was going on too, don't forget.

ALEX: Are there any more beers?

LILY: In the fridge in the cellar.

ALEX *goes out through the corridor.*

JUDITH: But honestly, everything in that time, that just seems like small fry to me, compared to the way the planet's going now. I know lots of things have got much better but the future looks pretty grim.

MICHAEL: Well, that's a defeatist attitude.

PATRICK: The climate's the big one, amongst it all. Who knows how that will play out, but it seems pretty clear that humans lack the collective will to do anything sufficiently serious about it.

LILY: And the capacity to do anything about it is considerably hampered by people who stand to lose a lot of money. Countries that stand to lose a lot of money.

PATRICK: It's not just money. If it were that, I think you'd see a whole lot of people who recognised that, regardless of the severity of climate change, renewable energy would still be the way of the future and there's an absolute packet to be made by being ahead of the curve.

No, I think unfortunately the idea of it challenges something deeper. For whatever reason, the idea of requiring change on that scale challenges a certain type of person's sense of self, their right to go on living the same life they've always lived.

JUDITH: You say that it's defeatist, Michael. I don't know, maybe you're right. All I know is I don't feel so much defeated as overwhelmed. I don't know where the struggle is, or how it's to be prosecuted. Perhaps it's just that I'm getting older and I'm more aware of why and how fiercely change is resisted, but it feels like the clarity we had then has just evaporated.

HANNAH: I don't know that it's just you getting older, Judith. I feel it too, that kind of not knowing where to turn. I think it's at least partly due to how nonstop the world is now.

PATRICK: We do what we can in the areas that we control, like getting the solar and grey water systems installed here and in Sydney, but knowing all the time that, really, it's a drop in the ocean. I find the thought of quite how harshly history will be compelled to judge our generation fairly galling, but clearly other people just don't feel it.

MARY *comes on through the front door.*

MARY: Could I ask for someone's help?

PATRICK: What is it, Mum?

MARY: Someone must have left the gate open, there are a couple of sheep in the garden and they've got a few avenues of escape so we might need a bit of a cordon.

MICHAEL: Sure.

HANNAH: I don't know that I'll do any sheep chasing but I'd quite like to watch.

LILY: The latch on the gate needs a bit of a fix, I've been meaning to get to it.

PATRICK, JUDITH, MICHAEL *and* HANNAH *go out.*

Do you want to see the sheep get pursued, Grandpa?

MARY: He's alright, he'll just be having a bit of a sleep.

LILY: I might give it a miss, I think they'll have it covered between them.

MARY: Yes. Well, tell me what's been happening for you this year, Lily, catch me up on all of your successes.

LILY: I'm not sure that there are many to speak of.

MARY: Oh, I'm sure that's not true. Last I heard you were doing very well.

LILY: That might have been a couple of years ago, Gran. There was a show I made with a couple of friends of mine, we made it to try and get back to basics, and it was quite successful, ended up touring around the country and won some awards. But, honestly, there's been nothing substantial since then. You think that maybe once you've done some good work you'll get some more, but it doesn't necessarily work out that way. I've been teaching a lot, though, which I'm really enjoying, I find it rewarding in a very different way. It took me so long to do anything in the first place, you know. When I was younger I was quite intimidated by Mum and Dad's reputation, which makes sense, I think.

MARY: But you always wanted to work in theatre.

LILY: Yes. Very much. Fatally.

MARY: I don't know much about it. What I mostly remember is how single-mindedly Pat had to push to get to where he is. Even when they were building this place, in the midst of all that, he still made sure to make his work and pursued every opportunity. It was like the single-mindedness he had about this place didn't at all sway his single-mindedness about his work. It was like he split himself in two.

LILY: Well, it was a different time.

MARY: I think as long as you're happy, Lily, that's what matters.

LILY: To be honest, Gran, I haven't thought about whether or not I'm happy for quite a while, and I think it's probably because I don't want to know the answer. I don't know what I'm doing, I don't know … why I got married, I'm not sure if I even really know the person that I married, and my younger brother's about to have a baby and I'm renting my parents' house from them and I don't know what to do about any of it, I feel like I'm just waiting for something, anything, really, just to … happen. I'm sorry, I think that probably wasn't quite the answer you were expecting.

She goes to the dining room door and opens it.

The sheep are gone. It looks like everyone's relocated to the orchard. Maybe we should join them.

MARY: If you want to, mouse.

LILY: Yeah. We can bring some snacks. There's a tray on the kitchen counter, that should be mostly ready. Just a pot of tea which is done … now. Okay. I might just put on a hat. Let's go.

MARY *and* LILY *go out the front door.* MICHAEL *comes in through the corridor and sits down next to* DONALD, *who wakes.*

DONALD: Hello.

MICHAEL: Everyone has this ridiculous notion that we're headed for calamity, that, as a species, we've dug ourselves into a hole we can't get out of, when all of past experience, all of history, tells us that, chances are, human beings will find their way around just about any problem presented to them. The endless inventiveness of humanity, yes, sometimes unleashes destructive forces, but from that often emerges great beauty. Think of the great works of art that emerge from the most terrible crises. Good art is never made in comfortable societies, it's not tolerated, it only finds its necessity *in extremis*, you know?

DONALD: Yairs.

MICHAEL: And sometimes when works of art have been forged in that kind of crucible they retain a kind of hard-won truth, but for the most part the work that we create is hollow, really, if we're honest, there's very little around in this country to aspire to.

DONALD: You'll have trouble with that.

MICHAEL: Well yes, it is difficult because it's exhausting. You question, you know, why am I doing this? Toiling away in what, really, would in most reasonable terms be classified as a dead art form, what use am I?

DONALD: I toiled on the railroads.

MICHAEL: Did you?

DONALD: I worked on the railroads.

MICHAEL: See, Lily never told me that, she's so reluctant to talk about her family, she's living in the shadow of them, it's appalling to me, to watch how someone is stuck by the shadow cast by those closest to them, I just want to tell her, bust out, you know! Who cares?! Who cares?!

DONALD: I think I need to use the loo.

MICHAEL: The trick of course about theatre, or any art, really, is making it real and relevant for us, you know, you're making theatre for an audience. So many people think that they can ignore this fundamental fact about theatre, you know, that it's about shared experience, that you are making this thing for people to watch, making something for other people, and you need to be attentive to that. Otherwise it's just wandering around in the dark saying whatever pops into your head and switching lights on and off indiscriminately, it's hollow. This next thing that I'm working on I think has the potential to be actually significant, it's not often that opportunities like this come along.

DONALD: Mary?

MICHAEL: I think she's outside. This wine is really excellent, actually. Say what you like about Patrick's work, his later work, but your son really has good taste in wine. I'm going to get another glass, do you want one?

DONALD: No thank you.

LILY *comes on.*

MICHAEL: Have you seen your gran?

LILY: She's with Dad, in the garden. Can I help, Grandpa?

DONALD: I daresay, you seem like a helpful lass. This fellow here might need your help.

MICHAEL: Do you want another glass of wine, Lil?

LILY: No thank you.

MICHAEL: Are your parents going to be spending any time at all in town between now and New Year's Eve? Or are they going to be here the whole time?

LILY: I think they're intending to stay here, that's always been the plan. It's their house.

MICHAEL: I know, I know.

ALEX *and* TOM *come on through the front door.*

ALEX: They've said nothing at all to you about moving back?

TOM: I asked Mum and she said that they weren't. Why do you care so much?

ALEX: They're dropping strange hints.

TOM: I don't know. I guess if they're coming back they'll tell us.

LILY: If who's coming back?

ALEX: Have you not caught up with this?

LILY: With what?

ALEX: Mum and Dad are moving back here.

TOM: Maybe.

LILY: To this place?

ALEX: Maybe, but they might also be thinking of selling it.

LILY: But we live here.

ALEX: I can't get a straight answer out of them.

LILY: I thought they might be moving back, but to live in town, close to Gran and Grandpa, not up here.

ALEX: Well, if that's the case, they'll have to sell either their home in Sydney, or this place. They have to get the money to cover the move somehow.

TOM: They won't sell the place in Sydney, they've just renovated it, Mum loves it. They've said that I can stay with them when I go back there.

ALEX: So it's here. They'll either move back here, or they'll sell it.

MICHAEL: We couldn't afford anywhere in town, Lil.

ALEX: But if they are, and they were thinking of selling this place, maybe that could be a good thing? It might give you and Michael a chance at something more permanent.

LILY: What do you mean, Al? If they did sell this place I don't think we can assume they'd pass on any of the proceeds to us.

ALEX: Of course we can't. But I think that they would want to help us. The way Gran and Grandpa helped them to build this place.

TOM: Maybe they've told Grandpa what they're going to do.

MICHAEL: You didn't ask them.

ALEX: I'm going to talk to Dad.

He goes out through the corridor.

LILY: What?

MICHAEL: I knew it, I knew that you wouldn't ask.

LILY: No, I didn't ask, because it's embarrassing!

She goes out the front door, MICHAEL *follows her.*

MICHAEL: I knew it!

LILY: If you want to save ten dollars maybe you could just have three less coffees a week, that would do the trick!

MICHAEL: I need my coffee to work!

LILY: Or buy a fractionally less expensive bottle of wine once in a while.

MICHAEL: You seem to think we're being unreasonable, we're not!

They go out.

TOM: How are you going, Grandpa? Holding up alright?

DONALD: [*tapping his head*] This planet sits on top of a strange universe. Could fall off any minute. That's something to watch out for. What a …

TOM: Mess.

DONALD: Yes, what a mess. Messy planet. Holes all through it. Burning holes all through it with matches, my mother would get quite angry, you know, wasting matches, only get so many in the packet. What's your interest in the game?

TOM: I'm not sure if I'm interested.

DONALD: Playing anyway?

TOM: Something like that.

DONALD: Good for you. I would always give things a go. How else do you know? What's your interest in this state of affairs? This belongs to you?

TOM: This house?

DONALD: Yes.

TOM: No.

DONALD: No.

TOM: No, it doesn't belong to me.

DONALD: That's a shame. It's a handsome house. Handsome house for a mouse or two.

TOM: I'm going to get drunk, Grandpa, would you like a drink?

DONALD: No, I'm quite content thank you.

TOM: My boyfriend left me earlier this year, and then I wasted the rest of the year and all the money that Gran—my other gran—left me. And I had promised her that I would put it towards something constructive, like paying off my debt from uni, which, Grandpa, hovers at about twenty-five thousand dollars.

DONALD: Not good to waste things.

TOM: No. Max left me because I stupidly, stupidly cheated on him. And I got herpes in the process, which everyone says is no big deal and to be honest hasn't bothered me since I caught it, but frankly the thought of it feels really, really shithouse. I really never thought I was the sort of person that would do that to someone else, it's a real shock when you learn these things about yourself. It was so stupid.

I feel like a complete waste of space.

I feel worse than that, I feel like antimatter, a black hole. That could have played some part in why Max left me as well. Hard to have a meaningful relationship with a vortex. I don't see a way of making things better. I really do need that drink now, do you want anything?

DONALD: Don't be too disappointed that you're stupid. We all start well but things tend to go wrong quite quickly.

ALEX *and* PATRICK *enter through the front door.*

ALEX: Would you ever think about selling this place, Dad?

PATRICK: Oh—

ALEX: It must have at least crossed your mind when you moved to Sydney.

TOM *goes through the corridor.*

PATRICK: Well, we didn't know that we would end up living there for thirteen years. This place wouldn't fetch as much as you might think, either.

ALEX: Well, maybe not ten years ago, but there's that big development on the other side of Chandlers Hill now, and—

PATRICK: Oh, God yes, that bloody housing estate. We drove past that on our way up here, I never thought I'd see the day when something like that was built so close to this place.

ALEX: Every city sprawls.

PATRICK: Anyway this place serves a good purpose, it's not as if it's idle. Lily and Michael can stay here, and you and Hannah are able to come up on weekends.

ALEX: To be honest, Dad, that doesn't happen very often.

I don't know, I just … If selling this place was something that you were thinking of, I wouldn't necessarily hold onto it on our account. I mean we love it, but really I think we want to try to be building something of our own. I don't want to speak for Lily and Tom, but … if this job doesn't come off for me that'd be disappointing. And concerning financially, you know, with the baby coming and … everything. But if I could just get a bit of breathing space, a bit of a start, I've got some really promising projects of my own and they could really pay off if I just had that chance.

PATRICK: Well, nothing's settled. Your mum and I are thinking of moving back here, so …

ALEX: Right.

PATRICK: It's still all up in the air.

ALEX: Sure.

PATRICK: I'm not keen on selling this place—

ALEX: Sure, sure, no, I didn't—

PATRICK: But let's talk things over.

ALEX: Okay. Okay, let's talk it over.

HANNAH *enters.*

HANNAH: There you are. Patrick, Judith sent me to look for you, she's wondering where the esky ended up.

PATRICK: It should be in the laundry.

HANNAH: She said she'd looked there.

PATRICK: How mysterious. I will investigate.

PATRICK *goes out through the corridor.*

HANNAH: Did you say something to your dad?

ALEX: I mentioned it to him. Just tried to get him to fess up about what their plans are. I think they haven't made up their mind.

HANNAH: Well … don't push it. Your poor dad, on his holiday.

ALEX: I just … the more I think about it, the more I think it could make a really big difference to us all. I don't know, give us a real shot at some kind of stability. This business we're all in, it feels like you're always getting knocked down and bouncing back, but I don't want to bounce back, I just want to … bounce.

HANNAH: Look, I just think we should be happy if they want to move back, whatever the circumstances. And if coming back to this house that they built is part of that, then … We're going to need all the help we can get. I mean time, support. Help with looking after this little creature every now and then. We're going to need that. Particularly if I want to think about getting back to work full-time at any point in the not-too-distant future.

ALEX: Yeah.

HANNAH: So let's not push them.

Pause.

ALEX: If I don't get this job we could be in real trouble.

HANNAH: You'll get the job.

ALEX: But if I don't.

HANNAH: Then we'll think of something. Things might not go exactly the way we want, I think we need to be prepared for that. Careers don't go in a straight line, you know, lives don't. Especially not in our business.

ALEX: I think maybe he didn't expect me to suggest it. They don't want to think that we don't want this place. And Lily and Tom, you know I love them, but they'll both sort of just roll along with whatever Dad decides to avoid really thinking about it. Tom especially. You know, keep things nice and vague. But what if it's not what's best for us all?

HANNAH: Well. It's not really our choice to make. Trading in this place to give us a shot at something … we can't expect them to do that for us.

ALEX: I don't … expect anything of them. I've never asked for anything. I just … hope Dad listens to me.

Pause.

Michael's driving me up the wall.

HANNAH: Don't let him get to you.

ALEX: Easier said than done.

HANNAH: Look, the guy's a complete narcissist, that's all. It's very boring, and I don't particularly like him, but he is married to your sister, and it seems to work for them. Lily and I don't get on all the time either, but we manage. I think I'm going to lie down for a minute, sorry, I'm just exhausted.

ALEX: Do you need anything?

HANNAH: No, no.

ALEX: I'll come with you.

HANNAH: I just want this to happen! If he's a late arrival I think I'm going to pull my hair out. Your mum was saying that you were two weeks late. It better not run in the family.

Do you think your grandpa's okay?

ALEX: It looks like he's asleep.

HANNAH: Should you—?

ALEX: What?

HANNAH: I don't know. Check his—

ALEX: Check his breathing?

HANNAH: Well …

ALEX: I'm not going to check his breathing, he's fine.

Grandpa?

DONALD *lifts his head.*

See?

They go out through the corridor. JUDITH *and* PATRICK *come on through the front door.* PATRICK *is carrying an esky.*

JUDITH: There was talk of a picnic on the hill for dinner. I feel like it's unlikely but I thought we should pack some things just in case.

PATRICK: Oh, I don't think it's going to happen, Jude, I need to drive Mum and Dad back into town in a minute, Tom's already gone for a walk.

JUDITH: Alright, well, we can leave this here and anyone who wants to can sort it out.

I think I'd forgotten how beautiful it could be, here. That bronze haze of light on the front paddock this time of day. I've no idea what it says on the clock, but this time. That sun. That's the time. You're a bit pink.

PATRICK: The sun got me yesterday. My shoulder's giving me a bit of trouble too.

JUDITH: Oh?

PATRICK: Just general creakiness, I think. Maybe overdid it in the garden.

She kisses his shoulder absently.

JUDITH: Poor shoulder.

Slight pause.

PATRICK: The kids know something's up.

JUDITH: I know.

I woke up early this morning, before you. Before anyone. Stepped down those stairs, through the corridor to this room. Could have gone the whole way with my eyes closed. I went up to the top garden, the grass was wet.

PATRICK: A night frost.

JUDITH: Yes. This time of year. The sun was just coming up. I've followed it all day.

To do the right thing by this small corner of the earth that is our home, as we had always wanted to. This small portion of a bruised planet. That old dream we laid aside, I can see how it might have a new shape.

So yes. Let's come home.

PATRICK: Alright.

They kiss.

Alright then.

JUDITH: You're driving your folks back to town?

PATRICK: Yes. Should get going soon.

JUDITH: Yes, it'll be dark by the time you're back as it is.

PATRICK: Are you ready to go back into town, Dad?

DONALD: Ready.

PATRICK: Mum was still outside, wasn't she?

JUDITH: Yes, she and Lily are sitting under the ash tree. I'll get her.

> JUDITH *goes out the front door.*

PATRICK: Okay, Dad, I'll get your things from your room, and then we'll drive back into town. Are you alright there for a minute?

DONALD: For a minute.

> PATRICK *goes out through the corridor. After a little while,* MARY *enters through the front door.*

MARY: Don, are you in here?

DONALD: I'm in here.

MARY: It's time for us to go home in a minute.

> *She sits down next to him.*

DONALD: I'm wet.

MARY: Are you?

DONALD: I'm wet. I'm sorry, darling, I don't know what to do.

MARY: Alright. I'll take you in a minute. I'll take you in a minute and then Patrick's going to drive us back into town. Just let me catch my breath.

DONALD: Is this your house?

MARY: No, dear, it's Patrick's, it's your son's house.

DONALD: I don't know whose house this is. I don't live in a house?

MARY: You do, dear, just not this one.

   Actually, you might be going to a new house soon.

   If you want to. Would you like that?

DONALD: A new house.

MARY: Yes.

DONALD: Don't waste anything new on me.

MARY: Oh, nothing's wasted on you, my darling. Only the best for you.

   Come on, let's get you cleaned up.

END OF ACT THREE

ACT FOUR: NEW YEAR'S EVE

About half an hour to midnight.

A party where half the people want it to be winding down and the other half want it to be in full swing. Food and drink are spread out along the kitchen table and benches. Most of the party is happening out on the lawn, with people periodically returning to the kitchen to refill their drinks.

The hallway door opens, slamming against the wall, and ALEX *and* TOM *enter, both quite drunk.*

ALEX: Someone stop him talking, please, someone, I can't bear it, I'm going to snap. It's relentless. He cornered me and just monologued at me, for ninety minutes, I hardly said a word. I was on the verge of telling him to shut up except that I don't think he'd even have noticed. I know he's unconscious of it—I hope he is because if he's not unconscious of it he's a fucking sociopath—but, Jesus Christ, it's unbelievable! Lily's always saying she doesn't get to see us as much as she'd like to and between us, he's why! I'm sorry you're bearing the brunt of this, but how the fuck did that jerk end up married to our sister? I need a drink, do you want one?

TOM: Yes.

ALEX: God, that feels better. To say that. I hate New Year's Eve. If I hear one more person say how great this year has been and how much they're looking forward to the challenges of the next and how grateful they are to have all their friends in their life I will throttle them, watch me, Tom, I will throttle them and put an axe in their chest. You're not looking forward to next year, are you?

TOM: No.

ALEX: Good, neither am I. Except for the baby, I am looking forward to that, don't think I'm not looking forward to that.

TOM: I think I'm getting a headache.

ALEX: Already?

TOM: I must be dehydrated.

ALEX: I'll get you a glass of water. There's a Panadol I think in the third drawer down.

TOM: In the kitchen? Thanks.

ALEX: Everyone's gone home before midnight. What a party.

TOM: Alison's still here.

ALEX: I have a theory, Tom, and I'd like to find out whether or not you agree with me.

TOM: Okay.

ALEX: I think that we are disappointments to our parents. What do you think?

TOM: I don't know, maybe you and Lily are, I feel like I still have a year or so's grace.

ALEX: Come on, Tom, yours is just a different type of shortcoming. By your age Lily and I had at least exhibited promise that we've failed to fulfill, you haven't even exhibited promise, just floated along in no clear direction.

TOM: I don't think it would be very fair of them to make a call about us just yet—Mum and Dad hadn't exactly conquered the world by the time they were Lily's age.

ALEX: They'd built this house, had three children and embarked on successful artistic careers. They were on their way. See the problem with theatre in this country is that there was still something for their generation to build—that room's not there for us, all we can hope to do is inherit their models, move some furniture around inside the structures they've built. A lot like their houses that we might one day inherit when we're decrepit ourselves. Our generation is a change of wallpaper. The ship is too big, too fast-moving to change its course. Unless maybe it sinks.

TOM: Well, it's not like they haven't helped us. They've been pretty generous to us so far. To you and Lily at least.

ALEX: Oh, come on, didn't Mum and Dad pay your rent through all your years of university? Dad still does your tax for you, Tom.

TOM: It all goes to an accountant.

ALEX: His accountant.

TOM: It's just simpler.

ALEX: It means you get off the hook of actually taking responsibility for it. You can't just pretend that money doesn't exist, Tom, or that it has nothing to do with you. In fact if you want to be an artist, which is what you want, really, isn't it, you just like to be coy about it, but if you want to be an artist then it's actually more important for you to be engaged with money, because you'll need to be across it to take care of yourself.

TOM: I'm fine.

ALEX: Oh, is it vulgar to talk about money? Well, maybe it's vulgar until you don't have it, but as soon as you don't have it your thinking changes pretty quickly. When you come right up to the edge you see how all it takes is a little push to tumble over. Anyway let's not talk about it, let's just pretend we'll all be fine because it beats dealing with what's real.

    Pause.

I'm just trying to look out for you, Tommy.

TOM: I know.

    Pause.

ALEX: I want a cigarette, do you want one?

TOM: I didn't know you smoked.

ALEX: Don't tell Hannah. Or Mum. Don't tell anyone. I don't smoke, I was joking, but I am going outside.

    He goes. JUDITH *comes on.*

JUDITH: Was that Alex?

TOM: Yeah.

JUDITH: How's he going?

TOM: I think he's having a good time.

JUDITH: He missed out on that job. He hasn't said anything to us, he doesn't know that we know. We had a friend on the selection committee.

TOM: Oh.

JUDITH: He was this close, apparently. Never mind. Your dad thinks it's a blessing in disguise.

TOM: He really thought that he'd get it.

JUDITH: Yes. Oh, I think I've had it. I'm surprised I lasted past nine-thirty to be honest, that's my bedtime these days. You've been so quiet since Christmas, dearie, I feel like I've hardly had a go of you.

TOM: Are you looking forward to moving back here?

JUDITH: It makes sense. With Grandpa the way he is, and Alex and Hannah's baby coming, and we're not getting any younger, frankly. And we do have unfinished business with this place, as it happens, not just your dad, me as well.

I thought that when we left that we would never come back and I was happy to think so. Life had become suffocating. Isolated. I wouldn't move back if I thought that it was going to be like that.

TOM: But do you *want* to, Mum?

JUDITH: Do you remember, Tom, how sad you were to leave this place when we did? You were so sad. I felt terrible about it. But I think it was the best thing for you, darling.

TOM: Yeah, we moved that time because Dad wanted to as well.

JUDITH: Needed to. I did. We all did.

TOM: Maybe.

JUDITH: What you're essentially suggesting, Tom, is that I don't know what I want, or that I want nothing, or that I feel my own desires are irrelevant, and that's not the case, and it's patronising of you to suggest it. If I didn't want to come back here, I wouldn't.

TOM: Yeah.

JUDITH: You might not want us to come back here and I understand that, but don't make it about me.

What do you want? Darling? From your life. For your life. Because, frankly, I find it very hard to discern any attempt on your part to—you're such clever boy, Tom, maybe parents aren't supposed to say so but you are talented, darling, and—look you don't have to do anything in particular but it is important to strive for something.

TOM: Maybe I'll get a schoolgirl pregnant and breed pit bulls.

JUDITH: I think that's unlikely.

TOM: Would you be ashamed of me?

JUDITH: That would depend on whether or not the pit bulls won prizes.

That was a joke.

TOM: I guess it was yours and Dad's plan all along to drag me kicking and screaming to Sydney when I was a kid and now abandon me there with nowhere to live.

JUDITH: Tom.

TOM: That was a joke.

Pause.

JUDITH: We were listening to the radio earlier, the fires are getting closer to here than they first thought. I've tasted smoke in the air all day. You can see them, a red smudge, if you walk out to the top of the hill.

The door opens, LILY *and* MICHAEL *enter from the dining room.*

LILY: Don't tell me to calm down like I'm hysterical, all I said was that maybe you should stop drinking.

MICHAEL: You said that I was harassing people.

LILY: You are.

MICHAEL: I'm having a conversation.

LILY: You're having a go at my dad.

MICHAEL: I am not having a go at your dad. Why would I? That's in your head, Lily, you're hypersensitive because you're so eager for his approval, so someone having an ordinary conversation seems to you like … Really, don't try to pin your own unresolved problems on me, I'm happy to talk to you about them but not when you're aggressive towards me because then it won't be a constructive conversation.

LILY: I'm not being aggressive. I'm speaking in a very calm and measured way, and I'm saying that even though you might not realise it, you were actually being quite obnoxious just then.

MICHAEL: This must be some kind of joke.

LILY: What's a joke?

MICHAEL: I don't know. This. I'm getting another drink.

LILY: Fine, but before you do I feel like it's my responsibility to tell you that you're getting fat and unattractive and that your sweat smells rank.

> LILY *goes out through the corridor.* MICHAEL *comes further on and sees* TOM *and* JUDITH. *He goes to the fridge, gets a beer, and walks out the front door.* ALISON *comes on from the corridor.*

ALISON: Alright, goodnight, Lily, happy New Year.

Goodnight, Tom, goodnight, Jude, happy New Year.

TOM: Goodnight.

> TOM *takes his drink and retreats to a corner.*

ALISON: What a lovely night. Not like me to be the last to go home, but here I am.

JUDITH: Well, lucky you don't have far to go.

ALISON: Yairs.

JUDITH: One for the road? I don't drink much these days but I seem to be making an exception tonight.

ALISON: Why not? It's not even midnight.

JUDITH: Tom?

TOM: Sure.

>JUDITH *pours them all a drink.*

JUDITH: To a new year.

ALISON: Hear hear.

>TOM *retreats back to his corner.*

Well, it will be nice to have you and Patrick back here, Jude, nice to get some help on the place.

JUDITH: The property is looking fairly ragged. Before we left, I made a big push to clean up the pine forest because all those trees had died after the fire. About twelve bonfires worth of dropped branches and kindling I piled up, and it's all still there, no-one's even bothered to burn it off.

ALISON: It's a lot to keep up with and when you're two people down it gets difficult. Oh, I feel like we've hardly had time to chat properly. You've had such a busy year, and your trip to Japan, I haven't even asked.

JUDITH: Yes, it was … very special, actually. A turning point. For me.

ALISON: How wonderful.

JUDITH: Oh, Ally, I wanted to talk to you actually, we've been hearing rats scrabbling quite a bit. Lily says she's been leaving out baits and the rats take them, but there are just more of them, which makes me think they're coming in to our place through the roof, from your place.

ALISON: I'd say there's a bit of back and forth.

JUDITH: Lily says you don't leave out baits.

ALISON: Well no, I prefer to leave traps because if a rat gets poisoned and goes outside to die, as they do, and a bird gets them, then the poison's going into the food chain.

JUDITH: I think the rat poisons they have now are a bit more sophisticated than what was around when we were young.

ALISON: We leave out traps.

JUDITH: Which the rats dodge and then flood into our place, they always have, for twenty years, because you don't clean your place.

ALISON: You don't clean your place all that much, Judith, you've not been here for thirteen years, dealing with none of the upkeep of the whole property.

>*Pause.*

JUDITH: Your house is an absolute pit and it always has been, and the rats only get in because you and Richard, in twenty-five years, have not completed the stonework on your side of the house!

ALISON: It's a big house in the country, Jude, if rats want to get in I think they'll get in.

JUDITH: Rats will go where there's mess.

ALISON: Oh, fuck this.

>ALISON *gets up to leave.*

JUDITH: Yes, that's right, go and practise your recorder! I hear you! I hear you through the walls!

ALISON: Yes, I am learning the recorder! It gives me great pleasure and it's very satisfying to learn new things!

JUDITH: Oh look, I'm sorry, don't go like this. Ally, I'm a bit pissed.

ALISON: Really?

JUDITH: I just struggle to understand.

ALISON: You've always tried to organise everyone else, Jude, you and Patrick.

JUDITH: I'm sorry. But I feel like I've got a point. Never mind. Just never mind. It's late.

ALISON: Yes.

JUDITH: Stay, Ally. It's nearly midnight.

ALISON: Alright. I'll see in the new year.

JUDITH: I'm sorry for being a bit of a dragon.

ALISON: A small dragon.

JUDITH: Yes. We should probably switch on the radio, see what those fires are doing.

ALISON: It's a beautiful night.

JUDITH: I know. It seems absurd that somewhere, many places in fact, in this little world, that terrible things are happening.

ALISON: Jude, I will go home. It's late.

JUDITH: Alright. And I am sorry for—

ALISON: Yes, me too. Goodnight.

JUDITH: Goodnight.

ALISON: Call if you hear anything about the fires, and we'll let you know as well, we'll have the radio on. We checked all the fire hoses and the pump the day before yesterday, so it should be all set to go if there's an emergency.

JUDITH: Okay.

> *They give each other a kiss and go out the front door.*

I'll see you up to the gate.

> HANNAH *comes in from the corridor.*

HANNAH: Come on, everyone, it's nearly midnight! Tom, have you seen anyone? I thought that they'd all be in here. Oh, there's your mum.

> JUDITH *comes in through the front door.*

JUDITH: Has anyone seen a packet of sparklers? We can't have New Year's Eve without sparklers.

> *She crosses and goes out past* HANNAH *into the corridor.* LILY *comes on through the front door.*

HANNAH: Let's gather in here.

> TOM *goes into the dining room.*

I'll get everyone. Alex! Michael, come into the kitchen.

> *She goes back out the way she came.* MICHAEL *comes in from the corridor.*

MICHAEL: Should we help?

LILY: I don't know.

MICHAEL: I can't talk to you, you seem to be angry with me all the time. It's hard to live with someone who's determined to be unhappy.

I've met someone else.

LILY: What?

MICHAEL: Nothing's happened.

LILY: So what are you telling me?

MICHAEL: I always said that I would tell you if I fell in love with someone else.

LILY: How noble.

MICHAEL: I didn't ask to. And you've been driving me away, things aren't—

LILY: Michael, don't worry, let's not talk about it. You want to leave? Okay.

MICHAEL: This is hard for me. I love you.

LILY: I don't think it's my responsibility to absolve you, Michael, which is what, in some convoluted way that I don't quite understand, you seem to be asking for.

MICHAEL: I'm trying to tell you that I still love you, but that something happened that I can't—

LILY: Okay. Something happened.

You're a good person. I don't want to go through this. I've gone through everything leading up to it, so let's skip it.

MICHAEL: Skip it?

LILY: Would it make you feel better if I fought for you? I'm sorry, but I don't care enough to fight, and it's not my job to make you feel better.

HANNAH: [*off*] Come on, everyone into the kitchen!

LILY: I guess we need to get a divorce.

MICHAEL: Yes.

> TOM *comes in from the dining room. It's clear he's heard every-thing* LILY *and* MICHAEL *have been saying.* JUDITH *comes on, holding a packet of sparklers aloft.*

JUDITH: Found them! I know it's silly but I have a weakness for sparklers. Here, everyone take one.

> HANNAH *enters with* PATRICK, ALISON *and* ALEX. ALISON *is at the front door.*

Here, sparkler for you, and you.

ALISON: Goodnight, everyone, I won't stay for the sparklers.

PATRICK: 'Night, Ally.

ALISON: Happy New Year.

JUDITH: Happy New Year.

> ALISON *goes off.*

HANNAH: Come on, it's nearly midnight.

> JUDITH *hands out sparklers for everyone.*

Does someone have a light?

> ALEX *pulls a cigarette lighter out of his pocket.*

Where's that from?

ALEX: Oh, I found it.

> LILY *lights the sparklers.*

JUDITH: I know they're a bit tacky but they're also beautiful.

HANNAH: Almost time.

PATRICK: And there we are.

Everyone is holding a lit sparkler. JUDITH *twirls hers half-heartedly for two seconds. They hold their sparklers in silence as they fizzle down to nothing.*

JUDITH: Well, happy New Year.

ALEX: I don't know that there's all that much to be happy about.

JUDITH: Oh, I don't know. I think it's going to be a great new year, lots of changes. Actually we might as well tell you all properly now, that your father and I are coming back here, to live.

ALEX: You're going to live in town?

PATRICK: No, up here, actually.

JUDITH: Yes, sorry to impose, Lily and Michael, but really, it's a big house, we can all live together for a while. Stay as long as you need to find a new place, I mean I'm sure by February—

LILY: You're moving that soon?

ALEX: Won't you need to sell the place in Sydney?

JUDITH: No, part of the bargain of us moving back here is that we're hanging on to the house in Sydney, we'll be back there fairly regularly for work, so it makes sense. It'll be wonderful. We'll be here to help when you and Hannah have the baby, I'm so happy that we can be here for that.

HANNAH: Jude, it'll be great to have you both here, really.

ALEX: Dad, I—Lily are you really sure this is what's best? I mean this puts you and Michael in a difficult position, doesn't it?

LILY: I don't know, actually.

ALEX: Tom, what's your interest in this?

TOM: I don't find it very interesting.

ALEX: Well, that's actually quite lazy, Tom, you must have an interest, because like it or not, you have a stake in this, it's your future as well. You might be able to finish your degree if Mum and Dad sold this place, you could use the proceeds to set yourself up properly instead of, well, flailing around as you have been. It could make a real difference to your life, Tom. I just think that this could be a family discussion and, and a decision's been made and we haven't even talked about it. We should be able to talk this through as a family. Is this what's best for all of us? If this is our inheritance, really, the difference it can make in our lives is now, not some far-off point in the future. Michael, you must have an opinion, you've always got one.

MICHAEL: I think that you should leave me out of it, Alex.

ALEX: I can't believe you're being so selfish.

JUDITH: Now hold on, we paid our dues. We lived in what you would probably call squalor for a number of years, and I am not complaining because it was our choice, but we built this place for you.

ALEX: Oh, thank you. Thank you for building this house that Lily and Michael now live inside like penitents, thank you for instilling us with this idea that poverty is noble, telling us how organic vegetables really do taste better and they're so much better for the environment, how amazing Japan is, well you can afford it!

We swallowed up this dream, this fantasy that you were able to spin but were wise or lucky enough to avoid yourselves. We'll never be able to build anything of our own, we'll just live in your world until you die and it becomes ours, and we will live in your home with your bones under the floorboards until we die. But we won't die soon. Because as soon as we can make our way we'll have to be supporting all you old people clinging onto life, lifting you above our heads in the manner to which you have become so exquisitely accustomed, wading into the sea as it rises around us!

And you've polluted and ruined the planet, but we're the ones who'll have to suffer, we'll be the ones who have to dig the human race out of that particular hole, if we can, doing our best to keep things less than completely catastrophic! That's the best margin we can aim for! And you think that our generation has a disproportionate sense of entitlement?!

PATRICK: We always encouraged all of you, every one, to follow whatever interested you. We warned you what a tough business this could be—

ALEX: You're our *parents*, for fuck's sake, we don't listen to what you say we follow what you *do*.

PATRICK: We've all missed out on jobs in our time, Alex, I think that you're overreacting.

ALEX: Have you even been listening to me? You don't listen, you're so used to telling everyone what to do you don't listen, not to any of us!

JUDITH: Alex—

ALEX: Dad, you said we were your life's work, yours and Mum's, well what a fucking turkey you turned out. I'm a failure, Lily's married a dud and let her career slide off into oblivion, and Tom's never finished anything he started and can't even hold up a conversation. Goodnight, everyone, I'm done. I do love you all, I do, but really, I'm done.

LILY: Michael and I are breaking up.

Everyone is silent. JUDITH *and* PATRICK *can barely conceal their happiness.*

JUDITH: Oh. Well. Alright.

Maybe then Lily you can take the downstairs bedroom while you're still here and we can move into the upstairs room and—

ALEX: That's my bedroom, that's where we stay when we come here!

JUDITH: We're not kicking you out, Alex, I'm not saying Lily should swap tonight.

TOM: Maybe I'll sleep in a swag next to the pool.

JUDITH *and* ALEX *glance at* TOM, *a little annoyed, and quickly look away again.*

ALEX: I think you're being selfish, I'm sorry, but it's just how I feel.

PATRICK: If you're in trouble with the house, then we can help.

ALEX: We don't want your help.

MICHAEL: Maybe I'll step outside.

Everyone ignores him. He goes out the front door.

PATRICK: I'm more than happy to discuss all this in a reasonable way.

ALEX: Discuss what? The decision's been made. No, no, everyone's made themselves very clear. I'm going to bed.

ALEX *goes out through the corridor.*

Happy New Year!

HANNAH: He's quite stressed. I think it's ... the baby and ... the whole thing. Life's going to be different and we're not sure what it means yet.

HANNAH *goes out through the corridor.*

PATRICK: Lily? Lilly-pilly?

LILY: Let's not talk about it yet. The sky's glowing. The fires must be close.

PATRICK: I'll pack up outside, check if we need to get the fire hoses ready.

PATRICK *goes out the front door.*

JUDITH: Darling—

LILY: I did just ask you, Mum, not to talk about it. It's fine. Dad could probably use your help.

> LILY *goes out through the corridor.* JUDITH *follows* PATRICK.

> *Suddenly alone,* TOM *begins to cry.* ALEX *re-enters from the corridor.*

ALEX: Tom?

> *Pause.*

Are you alright?
Tom?

> *He goes to him and holds on to him.*

TOM: I don't know what I'm doing. I don't know what I'm doing, Al.
Ever since Max left me my life's been such a fucking mess I can't lift myself out of it, it's like I'm on a train, this train in a tunnel, no lights, and it's going so fast I can't get off, and I don't know why, I don't know why I feel like, like—and I'm so stupid and useless, and who could ever, who could ever love someone so stupid and useless, a failure before I've started, I'm just so fucking *scared*. I don't want to be here. I don't want to be here.
I don't want to be here.

ALEX: It's okay. It's okay.
Oh, Tom. Oh, Tommy.
We'll be okay.

END OF ACT FOUR

ACT FIVE: NEW YEAR'S DAY

Early morning, outside the house. In the shade of a tall, beautiful ash tree. Nature is pressing very close. It's going to be a warm day.

ALISON *is setting up a folding chair, paper, pencil, and some watercolours. Occasionally she glances out to where the bodies of the hills opposite rise up out of the valley, the distant, winding track of bitumen road barely visible along the floor of the valley, obscured by a mesh of eucalypts.* MICHAEL *emerges from the house, carrying some luggage.* ALISON *spots him.*

ALISON: Off to Sydney then?

MICHAEL: Yes.

ALISON: No mucking about.

MICHAEL: Why drag it out? Hardly any of the stuff in this bloody house is mine, what I've got I'll fit in the car. I'll stay with my mum for a little while.

    I've always been curious about why you stayed here.

ALISON: Where should I have gone?

MICHAEL: You live in that crumbling, spiderweb-clogged house, you and Richard. You don't get many visitors as far as I've been able to see.

ALISON: We both teach in Hahndorf, you make it sound as if we're hermits.

MICHAEL: After all these years you still live like—

ALISON: Like what?

MICHAEL: I don't know. How you've always lived. With nothing. You hardly eat a meal you haven't scrounged the ingredients for from your garden. It's like watching a movie set in the Great Depression. This militant poverty.

ALISON: That's funny, it doesn't feel like poverty. I suspect neither you or I know much about poverty, Michael.

MICHAEL: What I mean is—here you are, still, while Judith and Patrick—

ALISON: Oh, I see. We stayed, they left. We didn't want to go, they did. We're different people, simple as that. Nothing very mysterious, Michael.

MICHAEL: Did you think that it would turn out like this when you started building this place?

ALISON: No. I feel old and obvious to say it, but the world as it is didn't exist when we were starting. Couldn't have seen it coming. Couldn't have imagined.

The strange thing is I can imagine, now, what the world will be, forty, fifty, a hundred years from now. I think we can all imagine it now, even the young. That's the difference.

MICHAEL: What do you imagine?

ALISON: A wasteland. With some exquisite, unjust pockets, like this one.

MICHAEL: I should get going.

ALISON: It doesn't look like anyone's coming to see you off.

MICHAEL: What about you? You're here.

ALISON: Oh, I'm just making some drawings of the hillside. I could draw it from memory, really, but I always get pulled back to this view. And it's not often we get a morning like this one, after there's been a fire close by. These red mornings. I heard on the radio that a few houses have been lost. All under control now, though, they think.

I should get to work, instead of nattering. Good luck, Michael, I'm sure you'll be a great success and go anywhere you want.

ALISON *sits down and gets to work.* TOM *enters from the direction of the house.*

MICHAEL: Morning.

I'll see you around, in Sydney, probably.

TOM: Yeah, maybe.

MICHAEL: Take care of yourself.

TOM: And you.

MICHAEL: And I've been meaning to say, Tom, that poem of yours that I read.

I thought that your poem was good, Tom. It's good. I think it's good. I don't like other people's work very much but I like yours. I hope that that's a compliment and that it doesn't make you hate your work, that someone like me likes it, but … Look, I'll see you around. It's a small world.

TOM: Where are you going?

MICHAEL: America. I'm going to make films. 'Bye, Tom.

TOM: 'Bye, Michael.

> MICHAEL *goes.*

> *After a little while, there's the sound of a car driving off into the distance.*

> *At some point,* LILY *enters. The sound of the car fades entirely.*

LILY: He's gone.

TOM: Yeah.

LILY: Well. That's that done then.

> HANNAH *comes out of the house, with bags.*

You're going as well?

HANNAH: Yes, we're dropping in on my family, and then home. Michael's gone?

LILY: Yes.

HANNAH: You might not want to hear this yet, Lily, but it's absolutely the right thing. Do you know what you're going to do?

LILY: Stay here, for the time being. Tom's staying as well, maybe for a few months, and then we'll see.

HANNAH: Well, we're just in town, so any time you need … I know that you and I … maybe we aren't that close but I think we'd be there for each other if either of us really needed it. I like to think so, anyway. 'Bye, Tom, see you soon.

TOM: Yeah.

HANNAH: Come and visit us in town.

TOM: Will do.

HANNAH: I think it will do you good, spending some time up here. Makes me glad to think of it. Alison! I didn't notice you there!

ALISON: I'm in disguise.

HANNAH: You are.

ALISON: I'm just doing some drawing, I'm invisible.

HANNAH: Well. Have a lovely new year. We're off. Alex'll catch you on the way out. Just tell him I'm in the car. It's too hot to be out, I'm going to crank the air-conditioning.

LILY: What?

HANNAH: I'm getting my insides kicked about, it's like he's rearranging furniture. Have a feel, Tom. Feel that?

TOM: Yeah.

HANNAH: If he doesn't become a footballer I'd be surprised. Although that would be a turn-up for the books in this family. Who knows? Who knows what your future will be, little almost-person? Alright, I'm off. 'Bye. 'Bye. Love you, happy New Year.

HANNAH goes. PATRICK *and* ALEX *enter.*

PATRICK: Don't worry too much about missing out on this gig. It's a blessing in disguise, I think. They'll have wanted someone who was going to stick around for five or six years, and that's not where you're at.

ALEX: I know.

PATRICK: And it would be very easy to get trapped being the servant of many masters, none of whom would have been yourself.

ALEX: Yeah.

I'm sorry about what I said last night.

PATRICK: Don't think twice about it.

ALEX: It was ungrateful. You and Mum are excellent. We're very lucky, all three of us.

PATRICK: Well. We feel lucky as well.

ALEX: Where's Hannah, is she—?

LILY: She's waiting in the car.

ALEX: Right. It's going to be a warm day. They expect to be setting a new record for January this week.

LILY: It was a new record last year.

ALEX: I guess records don't stand for long anymore. You okay, Lil?

LILY: You know I am. I'm okay. I actually don't expect to get any more upset than I am now. Mostly I feel relieved. Isn't that bizarre? Four years and the most I can feel at the end of it is relieved. You'd better catch up to Hannah.

ALEX: Yeah. We'll see you soon. Take care of each other.

He catches up TOM *in a big, fierce hug, then catches up* LILY *as well.*

'Bye, Ally.

ALISON: 'Bye 'bye, dear.

ALEX: Seeya, Dad.

PATRICK: 'Bye, boyo. Let us know if you need anything, I'm sure we can help.

ALEX: Yep. Alright, 'bye.

ALEX *goes.*

PATRICK: You've got a good spot there, Ally.

ALISON: Oh yairs, don't mind me.

She continues working.

PATRICK: They'll rattle off in a cloud of dust in a minute. We really need to have a go at the road, needs to be dragged, the drainways need attention. Might even need to bituminise the slope at the bottom of the hill. There's always more to do, it's never done.

This is my favourite spot on the whole place. The slope of the hill, the road curving away, the steep, rough pines, and that stand of oaks we planted, oh, twenty years ago, all of us, you kids jumping over the holes we'd dug as we worked. They've still got so far to grow.

I've always wanted to plant an avenue of oaks along this part of the road. I should. I'd never live to see them grown, but that's alright. Something for the future.

I know that none of this will last, that one day it will tumble into ruin and people will wonder what was ever standing here. But that's not for a while.

They watch as the car pulls away, rattles off down the road. Except ALISON, *they wave, all in the same way.*

I should get to work. I need to trace back that blackberry plant so we know where to rip it out. Want to give your old man a hand?

LILY: Sure thing, Dad. Tom?

TOM: Yeah, in a minute.

PATRICK: We can always use another pair of hands. [*As he and* LILY *go off*] I should draw up a list of things that need to get done while the two of you are up here, actually, before we arrive from Sydney. Maybe you could even fix up the fence around the orchard.

PATRICK and LILY *go.* TOM *watches the hillside. He sits down on the slope.* ALISON *continues to work.* JUDITH *enters. She doesn't see* ALISON.

JUDITH: Happy New Year.

TOM: Happy New Year.

JUDITH: Oh, baby.

Silence for a moment.

I do feel like it's going to be a good year. Maybe I'm silly to think so. It can't be tougher than the last one. Though I said that last year.

You know, Tommy, when you were born I prayed for you. I never believed in God, but in that moment I did need to pray to something. You came out with the cord around your neck, you were already dead, and they were trying to revive you, but nothing was working. For six minutes no oxygen was going into your little brain. And I just wanted to hold my baby. But I couldn't, I could do nothing, so I prayed. And they got you breathing, finally. But no guarantees you'd keep breathing, we were told to expect the worst. So your dad went and got a camera and we took some photos of this tiny life, thinking that it might be the last we see of it. If I look at those photos now I see Lily and Alex's solemn little faces staring at this brother they might never know. And they did let me hold you eventually and I could feel this … fierce little life in my hands and I was never, ever going to let you go. And with no oxygen to the brain for that long, you should have died, or have been severely, severely brain damaged. But my kids have always been lucky. You were my lucky last. And I prayed for you. You are a miracle baby. And when I was in Japan this year, and I knew you were so sad, I went into one of the temples, these ancient, beautiful places, where you can feel, I know it sounds silly but they do have this … energy, this vibration. And I lit a candle and I prayed, again, for the second time in my life, that my baby would survive, and I promised to pray every day if you did. I still don't believe in God but I do pray. Every morning, Tom. And I know I'm right to, darling.

THE END

Belvoir presents

THE GREAT FIRE

By **KIT BROOKMAN**
Director **EAMON FLACK**

This production of The Great Fire
*opened at Belvoir St Theatre on
Wednesday 6 April 2016.*

Set Designer **MICHAEL HANKIN**
Costume Designer **JENNIFER IRWIN**
Lighting Designer **DAMIEN COOPER**
Composer & Sound Designer **STEVE FRANCIS**
Associate Sound Designer **MICHAEL TOISUTA**
Assistant Set Designer **CHARLES DAVIS**
Stage Manager (rehearsals) **MEL DYER**
Stage Manager **LUKE McGETTIGAN**
Assistant Stage Manager **GINA BIANCO**

With
Hannah **SARAH ARMANIOUS**
Donald **PETER CARROLL**
Mary **LYNETTE CURREN**
Michael **EDEN FALK**
Alison **SANDY GORE**
Lily **SHELLY LAUMAN**
Tom **MARCUS McKENZIE**
Patrick **GEOFF MORRELL**
Alex **YALIN OZUCELIK**
Judith **GENEVIEVE PICOT**

The Great Fire is supported by Belvoir's program for young philanthropists,
The Hive, and has received matching support from the Macquarie Group
Foundation for donations made by Macquarie employees.

PRODUCTION THANKS Liam Murray, Ruby Mathers
PHOTOGRAPHY Brett Boardman
DESIGN Alphabet Studio

Eden Falk

WRITER'S NOTE

Kit Brookman

My deep thanks to all those who have contributed to the development and realisation of this play and this production, and to all those who are visiting for the first time; welcome, welcome, welcome.

I began writing this play three years ago as an attempt, through the prism of a single family, to chart a line from the social and political movements of the 1970s to today. What was the future the generation coming of age in that time imagined, and what is the one they've ended up with? What, in turn, do their children imagine of the future? What is the inheritance of a generation who thought that they could change the world when the political education of their children has taught them to believe the opposite?

A lot has changed in the writing of the play, and continues to change as I write this note in the midst of rehearsals. At this particular moment, years on from those beginnings, these questions feel pertinent; what is the imaginative project our society is engaged in? What are the qualities and capacities that bring us through crisis? How, when it feels impossible even to see the night from the morning, does one reach some kind of vantage point from which the future might be imagined? What might lie out there on that creaking horizon?

We live in extreme times. The past and the future call to us in languages we've nearly forgotten or hardly learnt.

A theatre is a place where we can listen.

Kit Brookman

DIRECTOR'S NOTE

Eamon Flack

This is a play about the struggle to imagine a future, which makes writing this note an odd experience. The thought that someone a few decades down the track may read this little book comes with the thought that this future someone will know what we don't – which is to say, are we doomed or aren't we? What will survive of our way of life? Will all this seem trivial? Or will you, future reader, be experiencing the same struggle?

To the future reader, let me give you a little context: The writer of this play, Kit Brookman, wrote it because he wanted to ponder what happened to the idealism and optimism and faith in humanity of the 1970s. The generation which came of age then – commonly called the Baby Boomers – are currently engaged in a sort of slow-burning showdown with the generation they spawned – commonly called Gen X or Gen Y (the distinction is blurry). For example, the week I write this – the last week of February 2016 – a political front is opening up over a peculiar tax concession related to property investment. We may well fight a federal election over it – though you, future reader, will know better than I do whether this turns out to be the case. This political front has its usual ideological and political conceits,

but it's underpinned by very real antagonisms between the younger and the older generations. At stake for both is the national inheritance. What will be passed on? How much of the good stuff enjoyed by the last generation will be enjoyed by the next?

The younger generation in this play are struggling with the sense that the old ways are corrupted and that new ways are unachievable. The older generation are struggling with the sense that they drifted away from their ideals and larger forces took over. Both are unsure of what to do. How do we imagine a future in a world where massive global forces, capitalist disruption and political demagoguery are the natural way of things? How do we impose our human-sized ideals on the monsters we have unleashed? How do we imagine a future?

Our political leaders are forever telling us that the only thing that really counts "going forward" is the economy. Only growth can save us. The future is a question of tax breaks, middle class welfare, budget repair... But a country, like a house, is nothing without the people and ideas than animate it. We're nothing without a way of thinking and a way

of being. Without language and
ideas. Without dreamy, squinting,
half-imagined intuitions about how
else, how *better* we might arrange
and live our lives. And these things
– our ideas and our ideals – need
renovating as much as our houses
do, which is to say about once
every generation.

The house in this play may well
be the country. It presents a small
model of the goods and ideas
that we pursue. It doesn't claim
to be comprehensive. It is only
about a single family. But the basic
ingredients are all there. Culture
and economy. Life and shelter.
Time to talk and to listen. A sense
of place. The struggle to find the
right words, to speak and be heard.
A sense of the larger cycles of life.
An urge to build something bigger
than one's own life, and to leave
something behind. The old struggle
against despair and exhaustion and
hopelessness. Art. Sustainability.
Love. Time. Place. A future.

Eamon Flack

BIOGRAPHIES

KIT BROOKMAN Writer

For Belvoir **Kit** co-wrote *Nora*, co-directed *Is This Thing On?*, wrote and directed *Small and Tired*, and was Assistant Director on *Cat on a Hot Tin Roof, Private Lives* and *Babyteeth*. Other plays include *A Rabbit for Kim Jong-Il* (Griffin Theatre Company), *Heaven* (seasons at The Old 505 Theatre and La Mama) and *night maybe* (Stuck Pigs Squealing). His play *Close* was shortlisted for the 2010 Griffin Award and the 2011 Patrick White Playwright's Award, and was presented at the 2013 National Play Festival. Kit was the winner of the 2012 Philip Parsons Young Playwright's Award (now the Fellowship for Emerging Playwrights).

EAMON FLACK Director

Eamon is Belvoir's Artistic Director. He was born in Singapore and grew up in Singapore, Darwin, Brisbane and Cootamundra. He trained as an actor at WAAPA from 2001 to 2003 and has since worked as a director, actor, writer and dramaturg all over the country, from Milikapiti on the Tiwi Islands to Melbourne and Perth. For Belvoir, Eamon has directed *Ivanov, Angels in America Parts One and Two, The Glass Menagerie, The Blind Giant is Dancing, Babyteeth, As You Like It, Mother Courage and Her Children, Once in Royal David's City* and *The End*. He co-adapted Ruby Langford Ginibi's memoir *Don't Take Your Love to Town* with Leah Purcell, and co-devised *Beautiful One Day* with artists from ILBIJERRI, version 1.0 and Palm Island. His dramaturgy credits for Belvoir include *Neighbourhood Watch, The Wild Duck, Brothers Wreck* and *The Book of Everything*. His adaptations include Chekhov's *Ivanov*, Gorky's *Summerfolk* and Sophocles' *Antigone*. *Ivanov* won four 2015 Sydney Theatre Awards, including Best Mainstage Production and Best Direction. Eamon's productions of *The Glass Menagerie* and *Angels in America* both won Best Play at the Helpmann Awards. Coming up in 2016 Eamon will be directing *Twelfth Night* at Belvoir.

SARAH ARMANIOUS Hannah

Sarah is a graduate of the Victorian College of the Arts, having most recently worked as a series regular on the upcoming season of ABC's *Janet King*. Her television credits include *Wonderland, Me and My Monsters* and *Home & Away* and last year she appeared in the Australian feature film *The Marshes*. Sarah plays the co-lead in the online comedy series *Fragments of Friday*, which was funded through the Screen Australia multi-platform initiative and is currently playing as a part of Qantas' in-flight entertainment selection. *The Great Fire* marks Sarah's debut at Belvoir.

GINA BIANCO Assistant Stage Manager

Upon graduating from the Production course at The University of Wollongong, **Gina** began as a Lighting Technician with Merrigong Theatre Company. Since then, Gina has worked with Belvoir, Sydney Theatre Company and Bell Shakespeare in a variety of stage management roles. Her theatre credits include Assistant Stage Manager for *Cat On A Hot Tin Roof*, *The Baulkham Hills African Ladies Troupe* (with Racing Pulse Productions) including their London debut, *A Christmas Carol* (Belvoir); *Macbeth* and *Romeo & Juliet* (Education, Bell Shakespeare); Handa Opera on Sydney Harbour's *Madama Butterfly* (Opera Australia); *Hipbone Sticking Out* (Big hART) and Stage Manager for *Life As We Know It* and *Catalogue of Dreams* (Urban Theatre Projects) and *Summertime in the Garden of Eden* and *The Unspoken Word is Joe* (Sisters Grimm). Gina has also just completed working with the Royal Shakespeare Company on *Matilda*.

PETER CARROLL Donald

Peter's distinguished career has spanned over 90 productions. For Belvoir he has appeared in *Seventeen*, *A Christmas Carol*, *Oedipus Rex*, *Old Man*, *The Book of Everything*, *Happy Days*, *Hamlet*, *The Blind Giant is Dancing*, *The Tempest*, *The Chairs* and *Stuff Happens*. His other theatre credits include *Krapp's Last Tape* (State Theatre Company of South Australia); *Chitty Chitty Bang Bang* (TML Enterprises); *Night on Bald Mountain*, *Happy Days* (Malthouse Theatre); *No Man's Land*, *The Crucible*, *The War of the Roses*, *Gallipoli*, *The Serpent's Teeth*, *A Midsummer Night's Dream*, *The Season at Sarsaparilla*, *The Art of War*, *The Bourgeois Gentleman*, *The Lost Echo*, *Mother Courage and Her Children*, *Victory* and *The Cherry Orchard* (Sydney Theatre Company). Peter has won many awards including Green Room Awards, a Helpmann Award, a Sydney Theatre Critics' Circle Award and an Honorary Doctorate of Creative Arts. Peter is the recipient of the Media Arts & Entertainment Alliance's Lifetime Achievement Award; he continues to be a proud supporter of the union.

Sarah Armanious
Marcus McKenzie

Sandy Gore

DAMIEN COOPER Lighting Designer

Damien has worked internationally across theatre, opera and dance. His designs for Belvoir include *Elektra/Orestes, Blue Wizard, Radiance, The Glass Menagerie, Coranderrk, Miss Julie, Stories I Want to Tell You in Person, Cat on a Hot Tin Roof, Peter Pan, Private Lives, Conversation Piece, Strange Interlude, Summer of the Seventeenth Doll, Neighbourhood Watch, The Seagull, Gethsemane, Keating!, Toy Symphony, Peribanez, Stuff Happens, The Chairs, The Spook, In Our Name, The Underpants, The Ham Funeral* and *Exit the King* (including the Broadway production with Geoffrey Rush and Susan Sarandon). Other theatre credits include *Suddenly Last Summer, Cyrano de Bergerac, The Effect, Children of the Sun, The Long Way Home, Storm Boy, The Splinter, Under Milk Wood, Pygmalion, Bloodland, Edward Gant's Amazing Feats of Loneliness, Zebra!, Blood Wedding, The Women of Troy, The Great, Riflemind, The Art of War, Ying Tong, The Lost Echo, Fat Pig, A Hard God, The Cherry Orchard, Summer Rain, Metamorphosis, Boy Gets Girl, Julius Caesar, Far Away, Bed, Thyestes, Morph, The Shape of Things, King Lear* (Sydney Theatre Company); *Macbeth* (Bell Shakespeare); *Doctor Zhivago* (GFO); and *Shane Warne the Musical* (Token Productions). For opera, Damien's designs include *Der Ring des Nibelungen, Aida, Cosi, Alcina, The Magic Flute, Death in Venice* (Opera Australia); *Peter Grimes* (Opera Australia/Canadian Opera Company/Houston Grand Opera); *A Midsummer Night's Dream* (Chicago Lyric Opera/Houston Grand Opera/Canadian Opera Company); and *Chorus!* (Houston Grand Opera). His designs for dance include *The Narrative of Nothing, Romeo and Juliet, Swan Lake, Firebird, The Silver Rose* (Australian Ballet); *The Director's Cut, Grand, Some Rooms, Shades of Gray, Ellipse, Air and Other Invisible Forces, Body of Work, Mythologia* (Sydney Dance Company); *Tivoli* (Australian Ballet/Sydney Dance Company); *Of Earth and Sky, Mathinna* (Bangarra Dance Theatre); *Multiverse, Be Your Self* and *Birdbrain* (Australian Dance Theatre). For lighting design, Damien has won three Sydney Theatre Awards and three Green Room Awards.

LYNETTE CURRAN Mary

Lynette is well known for her roles in Australian theatre, film and television. Her theatre credits include *Hedda Gabler, Cat on a Hot Tin Roof, The Chairs, The Laramie Project, Suddenly Last Summer, The Seagull, Aftershocks, Whore in a Madhouse* (Belvoir); *Medea, A Woman in Love, Martello Towers* (Nimrod); *Gross und Klein, Blood Wedding, The Crucible, The School for Scandal, Fireface, Pride and Prejudice, The Sunny South* (Sydney Theatre Company); *The Country Wife, Rookery Nook, Under Milk Wood, Six Characters in Search of an Author, Richard III, Just Between Ourselves, Ashes* (Melbourne Theatre Company); *The Day After the Fair* with Deborah Kerr (MLC Theatre Royal Company/Paul Dainty); *Presence, Tilly's Turn, The Boys* (Griffin Theatre Company); *Derrida in Love, Broken Glass, All My Sons, The Last Yankee* (Ensemble Theatre); and *Brumby Innes* (Pram Factory). Lynette was a regular on the television show *Bellbird* (ABC). Lynette's more recent television work includes *Cleverman, Wentworth, Rake, Bed of Roses, Wicked Love, Chandon Pictures, Always Greener, Stringer, Cold Comfort, Aftershocks, Love My Way* and *Underbelly: The Golden Mile*. Her early film roles include *Alvin Purple, Caddie* and *Heatwave*. She then starred in *Bliss*. Other feature films include *The Year My Voice Broke, Road to Nhill, The Boys, My Mother Frank, Somersault, Japanese Story, These Final Hours, A Priest in the Family* and most recently *A Few Less Men*. Lynette won the 1998 AFI Award for Best Performance by an Actress in a Leading Role for *The Boys*, the 2004 AFI Award for Best Actress in a Supporting Role for *Somersault*, and the 2004 Film Critics' Circle Award for Best Actress in a Supporting Role, also for *Somersault*. She also won a Sammy Award for her role in the ABC series *Spring and Fall*.

CHARLES DAVIS Assistant Set Designer

Charles is a Sydney-based set and costume designer and a recent graduate of the NIDA design course. Prior to attending NIDA, he studied architectural design at Monash University in Melbourne. In his final year at NIDA, Charles was thrilled to be a recipient of the William Fletcher Foundation Award for emerging artists. In the same year he designed the original productions of Stephen Sewell's *Kandahar Gate* and Michael Gow's *Writing for Performance*. He was delighted to continue collaborating with Michael in 2015 on a new opera production of *Hansel and Gretel* at the Queensland Conservatorium Theatre for which he designed the set and costumes. Other recent design credits include costume design for *Oh Mensch!* directed by Sarah Giles for Sydney Chamber Opera and set and costume design for *The Whale* at the Old Fitzroy Theatre, directed by Shane Anthony. He is currently designing the original production of Thomas De Angelis' new play *Unfinished Works* with director Clemence Williams and assisting designer Michael Hankin on *Lake Disappointment* for Carriageworks, *The Peasant Prince* for Monkey Baa and *Othello* for Bell Shakespeare. He is also thrilled to be working alongside Michael Scott-Mitchell as the Associate Designer on John Bell's new 2016 production of *Carmen* for Opera Australia.

MEL DYER Stage Manager (rehearsals)

For Belvoir **Mel** has been Stage Manager for *The Dog/The Cat*, *Is This Thing On?*, *Cain and Abel*, *Angels in America Parts One and Two* and *Every Breath*, and Assistant Stage Manager for *Ivanov, Peter Pan* (New York tour), *Cat on a Hot Tin Roof*, *Private Lives*, *Death of a Salesman*, *As You Like It*, *Neighbourhood Watch*, *The Seagull*, *The Diary of a Madman*, *Measure for Measure*, *The Promise*, the 2009 Australian tour of *Page 8* and the 2008 tour of *Keating!*. Mel has also appeared on stage for Belvoir in *Ivanov, As You Like It*, *Neighbourhood Watch*, *The Seagull* and *Keating!*. Her other credits include Stage Manager for *Lawn*, *Edgar*, *Remember Me*, *Legless* (Splintergroup/Festpeilhaus, Austria); *Roadkill* (Splintergroup/Performing Lines); *Underground* (Dance North/Performing Lines) and *Night Café* (Dance North), and Assistant Stage Manager for *The Golden Age* and *Boys Will Be Boys* (Sydney Theatre Company); *Masquerade* (Griffin/State Theatre Company of South Australia) and *Assembly* (Chunky Move).

EDEN FALK Michael

For Belvoir **Eden** has appeared in *A Christmas Carol* and *This Heaven*. His other theatre credits include *Macbeth*, *The War of the Roses*, *Gallipoli*, *The Season at Sarsaparilla*, *The Serpent's Teeth*, *A Midsummer Night's Dream*, *The Art of War*, *The Lost Echo*, *Mother Courage and Her Children*, *The Miser* (Sydney Theatre Company); *Who's the Best?* (post/Sydney Theatre Company); *Death of a Salesman* (Black Swan Theatre Company); *The Ugly One* (Griffin Independent); *A Game of You* and the UK tour of *Internal* (Ontroerend Goed). Eden was a member of the Sydney Theatre Company Actors' Company from 2006 to 2009. Eden has also appeared in the feature films *The Great Gatsby*, *Sleeping Beauty* and *The Daughter*.

STEVE FRANCIS Composer & Sound Designer

Steve has worked extensively in theatre, dance and screen.
His Belvoir credits include *Angels in America, This Heaven, Don't Take Your Love To Town, Babyteeth, The Book of Everything, Gethsemane, The Power of Yes, Ruben Guthrie, Baghdad Wedding, Keating!, Paul, Parramatta Girls, Capricornia, The Spook, Box the Pony, Gulpilil* and *Page 8*. Other theatre credits include *The Weir, The Sublime* (MTC); *Orlando, Battle of Waterloo, Switzerland, After Dinner, Vere, Mojo, The Long Way Home, The Secret River, Machinal, Sex with Strangers, Travelling North, The Splinter, Bloodland, Blood Wedding, The White Guard, The Removalists, Tusk Tusk, Gallipoli, Rabbit, Pig Iron People, Romeo and Juliet, The Taming of the Shrew, Embers, The 7 Stages of Grieving, Stolen* (Sydney Theatre Company); *Hamlet, Henry V, Much Ado about Nothing, Romeo and Juliet* (Bell Shakespeare); *A Rabbit for Kim Jong-Il, Between Two Waves, This Year's Ashes, Speaking in Tongues* (Griffin Theatre Company). For dance Steve has composed music for *Lore, Belong, True Stories, Skin, Corroboree, Walkabout, Bush* and *Boomerang* (Bangarra Dance Theatre); and *Totem* (Australian Ballet). Steve has also composed for film and TV. His awards include two Helpmann Awards for Best Original Score in 2012, 2003 and Best New Australian Work in 2003 as well as Sydney Theatre Awards for Music and Sound in 2011 and 2014.

SANDY GORE Alison

Sandy is a graduate of NIDA. Her extensive stage credits include *Small and Tired* (Belvoir); *Calpurnia Descending, Under Milk Wood, Uncle Vanya* (including US tour: Lincoln Center, New York and The Kennedy Center for Performing Arts, Washington), *Love Lies Bleeding, Scenes from a Separation, Morning Sacrifice, Amy's View, Medea, Les Parents Terrible, Gift of the Gorgon, Antony and Cleopatra, A Happy and Holy Occasion* (Sydney Theatre Company); *As You Like it, The Rivals, Electra, The Alchemist, Other Times, Summer of the Seventeenth Doll, Uncle Vanya, Pygmalion, Much Ado About Nothing, Coralie Lansdowne Says No* (Melbourne Theatre Company); *The Taming of the Shrew* (Bell Shakespeare); *Wit, Retreat from Moscow* and *Becky Shaw* (Ensemble); *Shellshock: Gallipoli Tortoise, Parramatta Girls* (Riverside Theatres). Sandy originated roles in classic Australian works, including *Jugglers Three, Sons of Cain* (David Williamson), *Kid Stakes, Other Times* (Ray Lawler), *Makassar Reef, Rooted, Big River* (Alex Buzo), *Daylight Saving* and *Chasing the Dragon* (Nick Enright). Sandy's most recent credits include, Channel 9's *Here Come The Habibs!* and the feature film *Now Add Honey*. Other film work includes: *Australia, Lorenzo's Oil, Evil Angels* and *Outback*. On television Sandy has appeared in *Rake, Murder Call, Farscape, Brides of Christ, Grass Roots, A Country Practice* and *The Flying Doctors*.

Peter Carroll
Genevieve Picot

Steve Francis, Michael Toisuta,
Gina Bianco, Charles Davis

MICHAEL HANKIN Set Designer

Michael is a NIDA-trained set and costume designer for theatre and film. His credits include *Jasper Jones, Ivanov, A Christmas Carol, The Glass Menagerie, Angels in America, The Dark Room* (Belvoir); *Jumpy* (Melbourne Theatre Company/Sydney Theatre Company); *The Aspirations of Daise Morrow* (Brink Productions, Adelaide); *Dirty Rotten Scoundrels* (Theatre Royal); *Of Mice and Men* (Sport for Jove), *247 Days* (Chunky Move/Malthouse Theatre/Netherlands tour); *As You Like It* (Bell Shakespeare); *Ugly Mugs* (Malthouse Theatre/Griffin Theatre); *Truckstop* (Q Theatre/Seymour Centre); *Songs for the Fallen* (Sydney Festival at the Spiegeltent, New York Music Theatre Festival, Arts Centre Melbourne, Brisbane Festival and TRS); *Rust and Bone* and *The Ugly One* (Griffin Theatre); *Obscura* (Force Majeure/Carriageworks); *Fool for Love* (Company B/Savage Productions); *Miracle City* (Hayes Theatre); *The Boat People* (TRS/The Hayloft project); *Judith* (TRS); *The Lighthouse, In The Penal Colony* and *Through the Gates* (Sydney Chamber Opera); *Liberty Equality Fraternity* and *Great Falls* (The Ensemble Theatre); *Deathtrap, Miss Julie, The Paris Letter* and *Macbeth* (Darlinghurst Theatre); *Suddenly Last Summer* and *Women of Troy* (The Cell Block Theatre). His short films include: *Reason to Smile, Julian* and *The Amber Amulet* (both winners of the Crystal Bear, Berlin International Film Festival). Michael has received Sydney Theatre Awards for Best Independent Stage Design for *Of Mice and Men* in 2015 and *Truckstop* in 2012. He has also been nominated for Best Mainstage Design for *A Christmas Carol, Angels in America, The Dark Room*, Best Independent Stage Design for *Deathtrap*, Best Independent Costume Design for *Of Mice and Men*, as well as two Australian Production Design Guild Awards. Michael is one of the Mike Walsh Fellows for 2016 and is currently Associate Lecturer of Design at NIDA.

JENNIFER IRWIN Costume Designer

Jennifer's costume design career spans 35 years across drama, ballet, theatre, opera and film. For Belvoir Jennifer has designed costumes for *Keating!, Gethsemane, Gates Of Egypt, The Laramie Project, Stuff Happens*, and *My Zinc Bed*, while other theatre commissions include *Stockholm, Soulmates, Up for Grabs, The Virgin Mim, Cyrano de Bergerac, Bloodland* (Sydney Theatre Company); *Don Parties On* (Melbourne Theatre Company) and the international box office sensation, *Dirty Dancing*. Her dance commissions include over 26 years of repertoire with Bangarra Dance Theatre, including *Lore, Terrain, Patyegarang, Ochres, Fish, Corroborree, Mathinna, Walkabout, X300, Uniapon, Bush, Skin, True Stories* and *Fire*, over 35 commissions for Sydney Dance Company including *Berlin, Free Radicals, Fornicon, Synergy with Synergy, Piano Sonata, Shining, Protecting Veil, Shades of Gray, Directors Cut, Ever After Eve*, as well as *Waramuk, Rites, Alchemy, Subtle Sequence Of Revelation, Aesthetic Arrest, X, Totem, Amalgamate, Narrative of Nothing* (The Australian Ballet); *Munjarli, Kulmuk* and *Game Over* (West Australian Ballet); *Oneiros* (Singapore Dance Theatre); *Protecting Veil* (Royal New Zealand Ballet); *Giselle* (Universal Ballet of Korea) and *Vast* (Australian Bicentenary 1988). Jennifer's designs for opera include *Romeo & Juliet* (Opera Australia); *Ainadamar the Opera* (Adelaide Festival Trust). Her commissions for film include the recent feature film *Spear* by Arena Media. Jennifer was also the costume designer for *Awakening*, the Indigenous segment of the Sydney 2000 Olympic Games Opening Ceremony, and co-designer for all costumes for the Sydney 2000 Olympic Games Closing Ceremony, the Official Commemorative Ceremony marking the Centenary of Australian Federation (2001) and the Olympic Arts Festival of the Dreaming Opening Ceremony. Jennifer received the 2013, 2014, 2015 Award for Best Costume Design for Stage by the Australian Production Design Guild and was also awarded a Theatre Board grant to study at La Scala Opera, Italie.

SHELLY LAUMAN Lily

Shelly works as an actor, writer and director. A Victorian College of the Arts graduate, she has appeared in productions for theatre companies including Belvoir, Sydney Theatre Company, The Hayloft Project, and Malthouse. She is a recipient of Keith and Elisabeth Murdoch Scholarship and the Gloria Payten Fellowship. Most recently, Shelly completed a Master of Fine Arts at the American Film Institute in Los Angeles.

LUKE McGETTIGAN Stage Manager

Luke is Belvoir's Resident Stage Manager. For Belvoir he has stage managed *Mortido, Seventeen, Elektra/Orestes, Radiance, The Glass Menagerie, Brothers Wreck, Once in Royal David's City, Miss Julie, Forget Me Not, Peter Pan* (including New York tour), *Private Lives, Death of a Salesman, Babyteeth, Summer of the Seventeenth Doll, Neighbourhood Watch, The Wild Duck* (including UK and Europe tours), *Namatjira* (Belvoir/Big hART), *Page 8, The End, That Face, The Promise, Scorched, Antigone, Keating!, The Little Cherry Orchard* and *The Caucasian Chalk Circle*. His other credits include *The Pig Iron People, The Give and Take, Bed, La Dispute* (Sydney Theatre Company); *Like a Fishbone* (Sydney Theatre Company/Griffin Theatre Company); *The Government Inspector, The Tempest, The Servant of Two Masters, The Comedy of Errors, The Taming of the Shrew* (Bell Shakespeare); *Paradise City, Through the Wire* (Performing Lines); *Alive at Williamstown Pier* (Griffin Theatre Company); *Scam, Abroad With Two Men* (Christine Dunstan Productions); *Flexitime, Market Forces, Shoe Horn Sonata, Blinded by the Sun* (Ensemble Theatre); *The Complete Works of William Shakespeare* (Spirit Productions); *Twelfth Night, Arms and the Man, Much Ado About Nothing, Spring Awakening* (Railway Street Theatre Company); *Barmaids, Radiance* (New England Theatre Company); *My Girragundji* (Canute Productions); and *Dog Logs* (Marguerite Pepper Productions).

MARCUS McKENZIE Tom

Marcus has worked as an actor throughout Australia. Originally from Tasmania, he graduated from The Victorian College of the Arts in 2010. Recently he performed in Xavier Le Roy's *Temporary Title, 2015* for Kaldor Public Art Projects and Carriageworks, and has collaborated extensively on new works with both Barking Gecko and Shian Law. Other credits include *Since I Suppose* (Arts House/Melbourne Festival/One Step At A Time Like This); *En Route* (One Step At A Time Like This); *night maybe* (Stuck Pigs Squealing/Theatre Works); *Beyond The Neck* (Red Stitch); *The Economist* (MKA/Brisbane Powerhouse); *Arquitectura de Feria* (Antigua i Barbuda/Sydney Festival); *Invisible Discourses* (LOVE/CITY Festival); *Pimp My Play* (Last Tuesday Society/GRIT Theatre); *Beautiful* (Tasmanian Theatre Company/Mudlark); *As We Mean To Go On* (Elbow Room); *Pains of Youth* (Artisan Collective); *Superhero Training Academy* (Tamarama Rock Surfers/Theatre Works). As a key collaborator of ARTHUR, Marcus has developed and appeared in numerous works including *Dirtyland; The Midlands; The Myth Project: Twin* (for Melbourne Theatre Company NEON); as well as co-devising the award-winning *Cut Snake*, which has since been published by Currency Press and toured Australia extensively. Marcus is a recipient of the Orloff Family Trust Award.

GEOFF MORRELL Patrick

Geoff is one of Australia's most prolific stage and screen actors. His stage credits include *The Blind Giant is Dancing, Ruben Guthrie, The Tempest* (Belvoir); *Australia Day, Rabbit, Away, Oleanna, Tom and Viv, The Seagull* (Sydney Theatre Company); *Vere [Faith]* (Sydney Theatre Company/State Theatre Company of South Australia); *King Lear* (State Theatre Company of South Australia); *Macbeth* (Classical Theatre Co); *Man of La Mancha* (Gordon Frost Organisation); *Speaking in Tongues* (Griffin Theatre Company); *Blithe Spirit* (Melbourne Theatre Company); and *Things We Do for Love* (Marian Street Theatre). Geoff's notable roles in film include *Ten Empty, Ned Kelly, Lucky Miles, The View from Greenhaven Drive, Coffin Rock, Gimme Shelter* and *The Mule*. His lead television roles include *Cloudstreet, Grass Roots, Small Time Gangster* and *Blue Heelers*, and guest roles in the series *Miss Fisher's Murder Mysteries, Rake, Winners and Losers, The Secret Life of Us, Stingers, Home and Away, Farscape, Curtin, Please Like Me* and *Serangoon Road*. Most recently Geoff has appeared in *Catching Milat, 8MMM, The Code* and the film *Red Christmas*.

YALIN OZUCELIK Alex

Since graduating from NIDA in 2007, **Yalin** has appeared for Belvoir in *Ivanov,* which recently won the Sydney Theatre Award for Best Mainstage Production, *The Kiss* and *Baghdad Wedding*. His other theatre credits include *A Midsummer Night's Dream, The Comedy of Errors, As You Like It* and *Cyrano de Bergerac* (Sport for Jove Theatre), for which he received a Sydney Theatre Award for Best Leading Actor in an Independent Production; *King Lear, Henry IV, Romeo & Juliet* (Bell Shakespeare); *Frost/Nixon* (Melbourne Theatre Company); *The Lost Echo, Gross und Klein,* which included a European tour in 2012, *Blood Wedding* and *Cyrano de Bergerac* (Sydney Theatre Company); *Shellshock* (Riverside Theatre); *The Importance of Being Earnest* (State Theatre Company of South Australia); *Vere [Faith]* (Sydney Theatre Company/State Theatre Company of South Australia); *Zig Zag St, X-Stacy, Romeo and Juliet, After January, Milo's Wake* (La Boite Theatre Company); *When the Rain Stops Falling* (Brink Productions); and the Helpmann Award-winning *Reflections on Gallipoli* with the Australian Chamber Orchestra. Yalin recently featured in two television series: Nine Network's *Gallipoli* and *Deadline Gallipoli*, starring Sam Worthington. He has also appeared in the feature film *Concealed* and several short films, as well as a number of radio plays, poetry and book readings for ABC Radio. He helped voice the computer game *Rome: Total War* and is also the central character in the web comic *Burger Force*.

Geoff Morrell

The Great Fire cast

GENEVIEVE PICOT Judith

Genevieve graduated from NIDA in 1979. For Belvoir she has appeared in *The Book of Everything*. Other theatre credits include *Small Metal Objects* (Back To Back); *Rock'N'Roll, Queen Lear, The Aunt's Story, The Rain Dancers, Miss Bosnia, Summer of the Seventeenth Doll, Arcadia, A Flea in Her Ear, The Sisters Rosensweig, Summer of the Aliens, On Top of the World, The Rivers of China, The Benefactors, A Midsummer Night's Dream, Top Girls, Who's Afraid of Virginia Woolf?, The Changeling, As You Like It*, and *Antigone* (Melbourne Theatre Company); *The Spook* (Malthouse); *The Great Man* (Sydney Theatre Company); *The Temple* (Playbox Theatre); *Wild Honey* (State Theatre of South Australia); *The Comedy of Errors* (The Church Theatre) and *Tales from the Vienna Woods* (Nimrod Theatre). Genevieve's film credits include *The Dressmaker, Force of Destiny, Muriel's Wedding, Proof,* and *Undercover*. Her television credits include *Miss Fisher's Murder Mysteries, McLeod's Daughters, Medivac, Bread and Roses, Wicked Science, Fast Forward – The Making of Nothing, Seven Deadly Sins – Wrath, Max Gillies – Vietnam Vets, Acropolis Now, Inside Running, The Four Minute Mile, The Petrov Affair, A Descant for Gossips, Timeless Land* and *The Sullivans*. Genevieve received the 1994 New Zealand Film Festival Award for Best Performance in a Television Series for *Bread and Roses* and the 1994 New Zealand Film Festival Award for Best Performance in a Feature Film for *Bread and Roses*.

MICHAEL TOISUTA Associate Sound Designer

Michael has worked in numerous sound production roles for theatre and dance companies in Australia. For Belvoir he has worked as a Sound Designer on *Windmill Baby*, as an Associate Sound Designer on *Toy Symphony* and *Yibiyung*, as a Sound Supervisor on *Once in Royal David's City* and as a Sound Operator on *Angels in America, Book of Everything, Exit the King* and *Keating!*. His other Sound Design credits include: *Masquerade* (Griffin/STCSA); *My Bicycle Loves You* (Legs on the Wall); *An Oak Tree* (Ride on Theatre/BSharp); *Framed* (DeQuincey Co); *Borderlines* (The Weather Exchange); *The Voices Project 2016: All Good Things* and *Max Remy Super Spy* (ATYP), while his Sound Supervisor and Operator credits include *Waiting for Godot, Uncle Vanya* and *Fools Island* (Sydney Theatre Company); *School Dance* (Windmill Theatre); *Conversation Piece* (Lucy Guerin Inc/Belvoir). He has also been a Sound Designer for a number of short films including *Hairpin* by Laura Scrivano (Dungog Film Festival 2011); *Jyoti* (Short Film Corner at Cannes Film Festival 2010) and *Woodlands* (Barcelona Film Festival 2007) by Carlos Marquez-Perez as well as the video art installation *Milk Ring* (Bridge Art Fair Berlin 2008) by Owen Leong.

SUNDAY FORUM

See the show, and let's talk about it afterwards.

Sometimes the most fascinating part of a theatre-going experience is delving into not just *what* it's about, but *how* it's being done. At Belvoir's Sunday Forums we bring artists and audiences together to peel back the surface and see what's really going on in our plays. We'll chew over the social, the political and the familial. We'll discuss the play, the production – and the glorious space between the two. Serious one month, feisty the next – but always intriguing and you're *always* invited.

We hold a Forum for each of our Upstairs productions. The panellists are made up of both theatre artists and invited guests; you can check our website in advance for a run-down of who will be on and the topic of conversation. You'll have the chance to ask questions, meet your fellow audience members and continue the discussion informally with us in the bar afterwards.

Sunday Forums are **FREE** but we'd like you to book so we can save you a spot. Book online at **belvoir.com.au/sundayforum** or call Box Office. Tweet while you listen using #sundayforum

The Great Fire
3pm, 8 May

The Events
3pm, 12 June

Back at the Dojo
3pm, 17 July

Twelfth Night
3pm, 4 September

The Drover's Wife
3pm, 16 October

Faith Healer
3pm, 27 November

Girl Asleep
3pm, 18 December

Shelly Lauman

Theatricality. Variety of life. Faith in humanity.

Belvoir is a theatre company on a side street in Surry Hills, Sydney. We share our street with a park and a public housing estate, and our theatre is in an old industrial building. It has been, at various times, a garage, a sauce factory, and the Nimrod Theatre. When the theatre was threatened with redevelopment in 1984, more than 600 people formed a syndicate to buy the building and save the theatre. Thirty years later, Belvoir St Theatre continues to be home to one of Australia's most celebrated theatre companies.

In its early years Belvoir was run cooperatively. It later rose to international prominence under first and longest-serving Artistic Director Neil Armfield and continued to be both wildly successful and controversial under Ralph Myers. Belvoir is a traditional home for the great old crafts of acting and story in Australian theatre. It is a platform for voices that won't otherwise be heard. And it is a gathering of outspoken ideals. In short: theatricality, variety of life, and faith in humanity.

At Belvoir we gather the best theatre artists we can find, emerging and established, to realise an annual season of works – new Australian plays, Indigenous works, re-imagined classics and new international writing. Our work travels the country and we regularly take our productions overseas. Audiences remember many landmark productions including *Angels in America, Brothers Wreck, The Glass Menagerie, Neighbourhood Watch, The Wild Duck, Medea, The Diary of a Madman, Death of a Salesman, The Blind Giant is Dancing, Hamlet, Cloudstreet, Aliwa, The Book of Everything, Keating!, The Exile Trilogy, Exit the King, The Sapphires* and *Who's Afraid of Virginia Woolf?*

Belvoir receives government support for its activities from the federal government through the Major Performing Arts Panel of the Australia Council and the state government through Arts NSW. We also welcome and warmly appreciate all philanthropic support.

belvoir.com.au
Artistic Director **Eamon Flack**
Executive Director **Brenna Hobson**

BELVOIR

JASPER JONES
2 JAN – 7 FEB

THE BLIND GIANT IS DANCING
13 FEB – 20 MAR

THE GREAT FIRE
2 APR – 8 MAY

THE EVENTS
12 MAY – 12 JUN

BACK AT THE DOJO
18 JUN – 17 JUL

TWELFTH NIGHT
23 JUL – 4 SEP

THE DROVER'S WIFE
17 SEP – 16 OCT

FAITH HEALER
22 OCT – 27 NOV

GIRL ASLEEP
2 – 24 DEC

THE TRIBE
19 JAN – 7 FEB

HANNAH GADSBY – DOGMATIC
20 – 22 MAY

RUBY'S WISH
21 SEP – 9 OCT

TITLE AND DEED
13 OCT – 6 NOV

2016 SEASON

COME AND SEE
SUBSCRIBE NOW
BELVOIR.COM.AU

NSW GOVERNMENT | Arts NSW   Australian Government   Australia Council for the Arts

BELVOIR DONORS

We give our heartfelt thanks to all our donors for their loyal and generous support.

CREATIVE DEVELOPMENT FUND

$10,000+
Andrew Cameron AM & Cathy Cameron **
Sherry-Hogan Foundation*
Kim Williams AM & Catherine Dovey

$5,000 – $9,999
Anonymous (1)
Stephen Allen
Anne Britton**
Hartley Cook*
Louise Herron AM & Clark Butler**
Peter & Rosemary Ingle*
Helen Lynch AM & Helen Bauer**
Frank Macindoe *
Doc Ross Family Foundation
Victoria Taylor**

$2,000 – $4,999
Neil Armfield AO**
Jill & Richard Berry
Justin Butterworth & Stephen Asher
John Cary
Janet & Trefor Clayton*
Michael Coleman*
Bob & Chris Ernst
Richard Evans
Lisa Hamilton & Rob White
Victoria Holthouse*
David Marr**
David Robb

$500 – $1,999
Helen Argiris
Richard Banks
Chris Collett
Joanna Collins
Linda English
Phillip English
Timothy Hale
Roey Higgs
Michael Hobbs
Stephanie Hutchinson
Angus Hutchinson
Alec Leopold
Janine Perrett*
Steve Rankine
Penelope Seidler
Alenka Tindale
Sheryl Weil

CO-CONSPIRATORS

$10,000+
Gail Hambly**
Anita Jacoby*
David & Jill Pumphrey
Mark Warburton
Peter Wilson
Cathy Yuncken

THE CHAIR'S GROUP

$3,000+
Judge Joe Harman
Marion Heathcote & Brian Burfitt**
Penny Ward*
David & Jennifer Watson**

$1,000 – $2,999
Antoinette Albert**
Jill & Richard Berry
Jillian Broadbent AO**
Chris Brown
Jan Chapman AO & Stephen O'Rourke**
Louise Christie**
Wesley Enoch
Kathleen & Danny Gilbert**
Sophie Guest*
Michael Hobbs*
Hilary Linstead**
Ross McLean & Fiona Beith*
Cajetan Mula (Honorary Member)
Steve Rankine
Alex Oonagh Redmond**
Michael Rose & Jo D'Antonio*
Ann Sherry AO*
Kim Williams AM**

2015 B KEEPERS

$5,000+
Robert & Libby Albert**
Ellen Borda*
Constructability Recruitment
Marion Heathcote & Brian Burfitt**
Don & Leslie Parsonage*

$3,000 – $4,999
Anonymous (1)
Bev & Phil Birnbaum**
Anne Britton**
Louise Christie**
Suzanne & Michael Daniel**
Robyn Godlee & Tony Maxwell
Colleen Kane**
S Khouri & D Cross
Chantal & Greg Roger **
Peter & Jan Shuttleworth*

$2,000 – $2,999
Claire Armstrong & John Sharpe**
Bob & Chris Ernst**
Cary & Rob Gillespie
Peter Graves**
David & Kathryn Groves*
David Haertsch**
John Head**
Jennifer Ledgar & Bob Lim*
Louise Mitchell & Peter Pether
Dr David Nguyen**
Timothy & Eva Pascoe**
Merilyn Sleigh & Raoul de Ferranti
Judy Thomson*
Lynne Watkins & Nicholas Harding*

$1,000 – $1,999
Anonymous (3)
Berg Family Foundation**
Max Bonnell**
Dr Catherine Brown-Watt PSM
Jan Burnswoods*
Mary Jo & Lloyd Capps**
Elaine Chia
Jane Christensen*
Tracey Driver
Jeanne Eve**
Lisa Hamilton & Rob White
Wendy & Andrew Hamlin**
Libby Higgin*
Michael Hobbs*
Avril Jeans**
Kevin & Rosemarie Jeffers-Palmer **
Corinne & Rob Johnston*
Margaret Johnston
A. le Marchant*
Stephanie Lee*
Atul Lele*
Hilary Linstead*
Professor Elizabeth More AM**
K Nomchong SC
Jacqueline & Michael Palmer
Dr Natalie Pelham*
Greeba Pritchard*
David & Jill Pumphrey
Richard & Heather Rasker*
Colleen Roche
Lesley & Andrew Rosenberg*
David Round
Andrew & Louise Sharpe*
Vivienne Sharpe*
Jennifer Smith
Chris & Bea Sochan*
Jeremy Storer & Annabel Crabb
Sue Thomson*
Paul & Jennifer Winch

THE HIVE

$2,500
Anthony & Elly Baxter
Nathan & Yael Bennett
Justin Butterworth & Stephen Asher
Dan & Emma Chesterman
Este Darin-Cooper & Chris Burgess
Joanna Davidson & Julian Leeser
Jeremy Goff & Amelia Morgan-Hunn
Piers Grove
Ruth Higgins & Tamson Pietsch
Emma Hogan & Kim Hogan
Nicola Marcus & Jeremy Goldschmidt
Bruce Meagher & Greg Waters
G W Outram & F E Holyoake
Olivia Pascoe
Andrew & Louise Sharpe*
Michael Sirmai
The Sky Foundation
Peter Wilson & James Emmett

EDUCATION DONORS

$10,000+
Doc Ross Family Foundation
Susie & Nick Kelly
Ian Learmonth & Julia Pincus

$2,000 - $4,999
Anonymous (2)
Ian Barnett*
Andrew Cameron AM & Cathy
Cameron**
Estate of the late Angelo Comino
Ari Droga
Matthew Hall
Julie Hannaford*
Judge Joe Harman
Matthew Kidman
Olivia Pascoe**

$500 - $1,999
32 Edward St
Anonymous (7)
Len & Nita Armfield
Art House Gallery
Victor Baskir
David Bennett AO & Anne Bennett
AB*
Michael & Colleen Chesterman*
Tracey Clancy
Karen Cooper & Simon Tuxen
Erin Devery
Diane Dunlop*
Veronica Espaliat & Ross
Youngman
John B Fairfax AO & Libby Fairfax
Geoffrey & Patricia Gemmell*
Dorothy Hoddinott AO**
Sue Hyde*
Peter & Rosemary Ingle*
David Jonas & Desmon Du Plessis

Stewart & Jillian Kellie*
Xanthi Kouvatas
Veronica & Matthew Latham
Ruth Layton
Jennifer Ledgar & Bob Lim*
David Marr & Sebastian Tesoriero
Mary Miltenyi
Polese Family
Angela Raymond
Peter & Janet Shuttleworth*
Nawal Silfani
Chris & Bea Sochan*
Kerry Stubbs
Drew Tait
Ingrid Villata
Richard & Sue Walsh
Andrew Watts
Carolyn Wright

GENERAL DONORS

$10,000+
Anonymous (1)
Andrew Cameron AM & Cathy
Cameron**
Ross Littlewood & Alexandra
Curtin*
Helen Lynch Am & Helen Bauer**

$2,000 - $4,999
Anonymous (2)
Baiba Berzins*
Brenna Hobson
Anita Jacoby*
Patricia Novikoff*
Lynne Watkins & Nicolas Harding

$500 - $1,999
Anonymous (5)
Victor Baskir
Christine Bishop

Ian Breden & Josephine Key*
Angela Browne
Dr & Mrs Gil Burton
Trevor Carroll
Tim & Bryony Cox*
Jane Diamond*
Elizabeth Fairfax
Jono Gavin
Peter Gray & Helen Thwaites
Priscilla Guest*
Kim Harding & Irene Miller
Harrison & Kate Higgs*
Dorothy Hoddinott AO**
Iphygenia Kallinikos
Robert Kidd
Daniel Knight
Wolf Krueger & José Gutierrez*
Frans Lauenstein
Dr David and Barbara Millons
Irena Nebenzahl
Anthony Nugent*
Judy & Geoff Patterson*
Dr Natalie Pelham
Kathirasen Ponnusamy*
Leigh Sanderson
Elfriede Sangkuhl
Abhijit & Janice Sengupta
Dr Agnes Sinclair
Eileen Slarke & Family*
Andrew Smyth-Kirk
Dr Titia Sprague
Paul Stein
Mike Thompson
Suzanne & Ross Tzannes AM*
Jane Uebergang
Louise & Steve Verrier
Chris Vik & Chelsea Albert
Sarah Walters*
Louisa Ward & Tim Coen
Brian & Trish Wright

* 5+ years of giving   ** 10+ years of giving   *** 15+ years of giving

Belvoir is very grateful to accept all donations. Donations over $2 are tax deductible. If you would like to make a donation or would like further information about any of our donor programs please call our Development Team on 02 9698 3344 or email development@belvoir.com.au

List correct at time of printing.

SPECIAL THANKS

We would like to acknowledge Cajetan Mula, Len Armfield and Geoffrey Scharer. They will always be remembered for their generosity to Belvoir.

These people and foundations supported the redevelopment of Belvoir Street Theatre and purchase of our warehouse.
Andrew & Cathy Cameron (refurbishment of theatre & warehouse)
Russell Crowe (Downstairs Theatre & purchase of warehouse)
The Gonski Foundation & The Nelson Meers Foundation (Gonski Meers Foyer)
Andrew & Wendy Hamlin (Brenna's office)
Hal Herron (The Hal Bar)
Geoffrey Rush (redevelopment of theatre)
Fred Street AM (Upstairs Dressing Room)

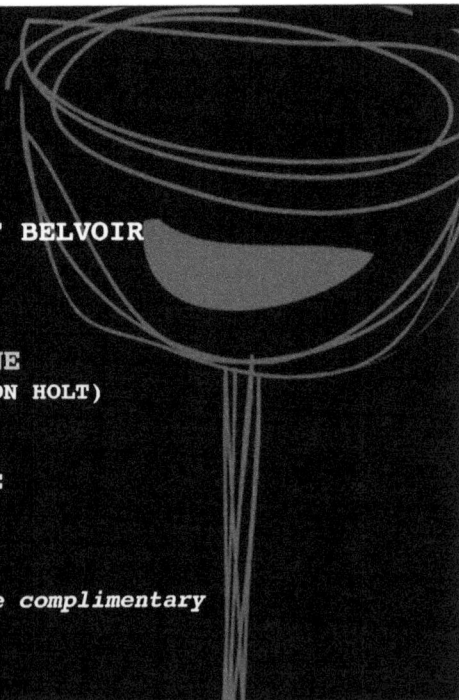

BELVOIR SPONSORS

MAJOR SPONSORS

EY Building a better working world

{ WOOLCOTT RESEARCH

BAKER & McKENZIE

MEDIA PARTNERS

SBS

WORLD MOVIES

IT PARTNER

NCC

ASSOCIATE SPONSORS

REGENTS COURT
BOUTIQUE ACCOMMODATION

barton deakin
Government Relations

KEY SUPPORTER

THE BALNAVES FOUNDATION

Indigenous theatre at Belvoir supported by The Balnaves Foundation

EVENT SPONSORS

VINI

the devonshire

CELLARMASTERS

Coopers

HUNTER VALLEY Stays
UNIQUE ACCOMMODATION

bourke street bakery

zahli

Hatrick Catering

~ MOHR ~

GOVERNMENT PARTNERS

Australian Government | Australia Council for the Arts

NSW GOVERNMENT | Arts NSW

YOUTH & EDUCATION SUPPORTERS

Man

ACTT | Actors College of Theatre & Television

TRUSTS & FOUNDATIONS

AMP Foundation
Copyright Agency Ltd
Coca-Cola Australia Foundation
Crown Resorts Foundation

Gandevia Foundation
The Greatorex Foundation
Thyne Reid Foundation
Vincent Fairfax Family Foundation

SUPPORTERS

Macquarie Group
Thomas Creative
Time Out Australia

PRODUCTION SUPPORTERS

MACQUARIE

the hive

For more information on partnership opportunities please contact our Development team on 02 9698 3344 or email development@belvoir.com.au

Correct at time of printing.